READ HOW WE DIED

by
Andrea Grieveson

CON-PSY PUBLICATIONS MIDDLESEX

First Edition

© Andrea Grieveson
1996

Published by

CON-PSY PUBLICATIONS

22 KINGSLEY AVENUE
SOUTHALL
MIDDLESEX UB1 2NA

ISBN 1 898680 07 8

Back cover photograph by Robert Crumpton.

CONTENTS

INTRODUCTION

Everyone in the world, at some time in their life, wonders about death and dying.

If you have been bereaved yourself, you have such a desolate feeling of ignorance as to how the person felt just before their death. Is there really something after death? How does one get to it? What is it? Is there scenery and countryside? Are there relatives waiting to greet you? Will you feel strange and frightened? What about Hell? Does it exist? Are you judged on your life? Are there angels?

So many questions and so few answers.

Although for the most part, we do not dwell on this morbid subject, when someone you know and care for dies - somehow death has much more significance, and your life is never really the same again. Somehow you have to cope alone with little or no information to help you.

'Read How We Died' is a collection of experiences, written through the mediumship of Andrea Grieveson. Ordinary people have put in great efforts of concentration in order to contact you and to tell their own individual stories of before, during, and after the moment we call death. They want to enlighten and inform you.

The stories are simple and mostly told by each person as they remember it. Their lives were like yours and the lives of the majority of people around the world.

The experiences are related here in a subtle style which deals with an often frightening situation in a way that takes you through each experience, involved - yet detached. Somehow the emotions do not become out of hand, and the reader feels the whole experience objectively. The aim of these communicators is to bring you knowledge and most of all - comfort.

FOREWORD

I never thought of myself as anything but an ordinary, down to earth Yorkshire woman. My interests were my family, business and playing competitive bridge. My two children Tim and Sophie kept me very busy while I was helping my husband to run a small supermarket in Hull.

I had no interest in psychic matters at all until about the age of forty, although I had always been a bit intuitive. For no reason that I can explain, when I was housebound, suffering acute sciatica, I asked Tim to get me some library books on Reincarnation. He came back with three, which I began to read with interest accompanied by a very peculiar feeling of familiarity. When I got better, I felt impelled to investigate life after death.

It was during this investigation that I met Alan - and had anyone told me then, that I would eventually marry him, I would have thought them potty!

One Sunday evening, with my friend Shirley, I visited the Psychic Centre in Hull, to see for the first time, a trance medium. Frank Grieveson, Alan's father, had been a trance medium for several years, and that Sunday, as his total personality underwent a dramatic change from that of an ordinary man, with a distinct North Yorkshire accent, into a cultured, Oxford scientist - I knew that there was something after death. I felt a distinct connection with this spirit who was speaking through Frank's body.

I had some private sittings at the Grieveson's, and was invited to sit in Dorothy Grieveson's private development circle. My interests and my life started to change over the months, and a couple of years later, I was divorced and Alan and I were married.

In 1980 Alan and I sat to develop. To us this meant withdrawing for an hour or so from the physical world; relaxing and playing music. Trying not to think about our daily lives and problems. Of course we didn't realise then that we were, in fact, raising our conscious awareness on to a different level. By

5

not focussing our thoughts on our world, we became more in tune with the non-physical world and our spiritual selves.

Our hope was for Alan to develop a trance mediumship, like his father. I didn't think that I, too was developing. Several psychic things had happened to me just before I got sciatica, and I suppose they had helped bring about the great changes I would make in my life.

About a year later, one evening, a voice pushed through Alan's state of drowsiness, and excited, I pressed the button of the tape recorder. Only one or two words were spoken on that first occasion - but spoken with a very strong foreign accent. Every night the communications became longer as different people introduced themselves.

Of course we were very happy and there began a relationship between ourselves and a large group of what are known as 'spirit people'. Over the years I have had hundreds of conversations with people who have, I believe, died. Many of these communicators have become almost a part of our family - interested in our lives, and, when asked, they will offer guidance and ideas for us to ponder.

Whenever I stopped to think about this ongoing communication, I always thought the same thing - how absolutely amazing it all was. I still think that sixteen years later.

We eventually opened the trance mediumship to friends and people who needed guidance, and also started a group, meeting fortnightly to hear a trance address and later to discuss what had been said. This group lasted for two years, then we moved away to sample life in a different part of the country.

Over the years we have done a little of what is called 'rescue' work - all under the control of those on the other side. It seems that at times it is easier for them to link to those they are trying to help, through us in the physical world. I have included in this book the transcripts of four of my husbands 'Rescue' tapes, to give you an idea of what happens.

One tape is of Jack, an old Yorkshire man who came along to tell us how he had died, quite a few years earlier. It seems that his coming along to talk about it actually helped his further progress in his world. Maybe it was the fact that he could look at it all in a more detached manner, without getting emotionally uptight, that showed his spiritual progress.

A second tape concerns Matthew, a Londoner who had died, but would not accept the fact. He was what is known as 'earthbound'. There is also a sequel to this attempt at 'rescuing' Matthew, which occurred six months later, and which I have included here.

The third tape I want you to read, concerns Archie, who died in Chicago in the late nineteen forties. I really enjoyed talking to Archie, and I feel I learned much from him. The biggest difficulty I had with him, was trying to convince him that I was actually alive and living in England as we spoke!

Richard is the subject of the fourth tape. His case is somewhat different because, due to his very negative way of life, several hundred years ago, his after-death experience was very different from the others.

The rest of the book concerns my own personal evidence.

I had always regarded my husband's mediumship as far superior to anything I was getting, but I found that I was in fact developing quite a lot. I knew many things about our life and the lives of others that I could not have known by physical means. I began seeing some people in past experiences and situations, and I came to realise that reincarnation must not only be feasible, but necessary, if we are to improve spiritually through physical experiences.

With a friend, I met a couple she knew, and I got the feeling they had previously incarnated in Finland. It was fascinating to hear them tell my friend they had just come back from a holiday there! The past lives I picked up on always had some connection with this current life.

Then, about four years after we had moved to Bradford, I felt the urge to sit at the word processor, because someone wanted to write something through me, about how they had died.

I must admit that I did nothing about it for a few weeks. It was my way of testing that it was, really someone else and not myself. The idea kept coming so eventually I sat in front of the keyboard and tried to quieten my thoughts. A sentence came into my head but I ignored it, thinking it was just a product of my own, but, as it kept coming back, I decided to type it.

From then on words just flowed and the stories came along very quickly. Except that they were all dead, I felt that the communicators were all very different - some seemed to take a strong hold, like a very efficient boss dictating a letter, and others were so gentle that I used to ask them to be more emphatic.

During the typing I always felt a kind of knot in my stomach - I think this was my own resistance to these people coming along and tuning in with my mind.

Taking down the stories has been very interesting. In no case had I any idea of what they were going to write. I was quite skeptical at the start, mentally criticising in advance what might be the outcome - but I was always proved wrong! I think I gave the early communicators a difficult time, constantly interrupting their flow and doubting before the end!

I feel that I have learned much from the whole experience, because, like everyone else, I have often wondered what it must be like to die.

The most important thing these people have taught me, is that no two individuals ever have an identical experience - whether they are dying or just watching a film.

I hope that you, too, will derive benefit from sharing these experiences.

PART ONE

Part One is the largest section in the book. It deals with accidents in which people died.

I remember, when I used to pedal my bike to work in my first job, that if I passed any road accident, it always spoiled my day. I would sit at work imagining how the accident could have happened, and whether the person had been killed or seriously injured. Like most people I always put the worst interpretation on what I had seen. When later I was involved in a road accident myself, it put a whole new perspective on the subject. I was knocked unconscious and remembered nothing at all - even though my body sustained a lot of damage and the blood was really flowing!

I have put Alec's story first because he actually tells us about this human tendency to believe the worst.

All of the following experiences throw some light on those daily accidents we encounter, see on TV, or read about.

ALEC

It was a marvellous match. Our side was winning by a goal, but the others looked as though they had plenty in them yet, so it wasn't the end, even though there were only ten minutes to go.

The excitement was building both on the field and in the stands, and I could feel the hairs on my neck standing on end a bit as the ripples ran through the crowd.

Then their centre made a break and took the ball away off down the middle, being well covered by our man. He passed the ball to his wing out on his right, ran fast up field, received the ball back and just shot it fairly and squarely into the net.

The crowd went mad, and there was an almighty surge

forward- it must have started from the very back row - and, just like a tremendous wave, bodies came hurtling down.

I didn't really know what had hit me. The excitement in the air - as well as that I felt myself at the closing minutes of a good, fast football match, masked everything. I felt the breath being driven from my body - a sharp searing pain in my chest and my head felt like it would burst - and then nothing.

Imagine my amazement, when I found myself lying on the ground and the whole stadium empty! I got to my feet wondering just what I was doing on the ground. I felt fine. What the heck had happened to me - I must have fainted. My legs were all right and I had no trouble walking, so I set off home, puzzling over why I had been left by everyone. Maybe I had waited for the crowd to clear a bit instead of getting pushed and pulled in the stampede out of the gates. Then perhaps I had just collapsed when they had all gone. It was very strange, but never mind, I was fine now and I could go and get my car and get home for tea, then a wash and feet up for a night's telly. The thoughts of it all made me feel quite cheerful. I whistled as I made my way to the car park.

There was no sign of my car. The car park was completely deserted. 'I had better get round to the police station, I think and report my car stolen. What a devil that was! I might not get it back for Monday', I thought. Well, I'll have to hire one if not. I knew the police station wasn't too far from the stadium and walked briskly as it was starting to get a bit dark now.

The bobby at the desk was quite a young looking chap, and I walked in and stood waiting for him to come off the phone.

He was talking about a disaster at the football ground that day. I listened in with interest and heard that twenty people had been crushed to death and it had taken the police and ambulance an hour to clear the ground. I looked at my watch for the first time and saw it was eight o'clock. Good Lord! Mary was going to be a bit worried! I coughed and stared at the bobby to try to get him to end his conversation and see to me. However he went on talking as if he hadn't heard me, so I

10

decided to speak to him.

'I'm sorry to interrupt you, but can you help me - my car has been stolen?'

He just went on talking on the phone and completely ignored me. I started to get a bit angry as I was worried now about Mary. I banged on the counter with my fist - at least that's what I intended to do but there was no counter there - my fist just went on down through the air. I felt the counter with both hands and it was uncanny - it was just space - nothing!

I decided to get hold of the bobby's arm as he held the phone, and you can imagine my feelings when there was no arm - I could feel nothing!

By now I was starting to panic. I just didn't know what was going on and I thought of Mary again and wished I was home with her.

It was like Aladdin! No sooner had I thought than I was actually there - at my house, in the living room where Mary was sitting on the settee, crying. With her was her mother and my mother and father. They all looked bad - very upset.

I went over to Mary and knelt down to her. She was not a woman who cried a lot and seeing it really upset me. The shock was that I had the same result as in the police station. Mary was not there to my touch. She neither saw nor heard me either. I had no idea what was happening to me and I was absolutely powerless to comfort my wife.

Then my father spoke and suggested Mary went to bed and had our doctor round to give her a sedative. The mothers seemed to agree and bustled about to achieve this. Not knowing what else to do, I sat down where Mary had been on the settee. My father had phoned for the doctor and then sat down opposite to me in the armchair. I looked hard at him and thought 'Oh Dad, I wish you could hear me!'

'I can son.'

I could hardly believe it! I got up and went over to him.

'You can hear me, Dad?'

'Yes. You know I am a medium son, don't you? It's no secret when I work at the Spiritualist church!'

'What are you saying Dad?' I asked him, not really

11

wanting to hear his answer.

'I'm afraid you've been killed, son. In the crush at the football ground. Didn't you realise it?'

'No.' I said. Then I thought about it all for a minute or two. 'But when I really think about it, I realise it must be true.'

I sat back down. This was a bit of a shock and Dad suddenly disappeared from my sight and the world went black again.

It seems I was quite a long time coming to accept my death. I stayed in a self-induced comatose state in which I knew nothing - just like a very deep sleep.

Then I woke up. I opened my eyes as I had felt a close presence of someone. I was sitting on a mound of grass, with my back against a smooth upright stone. Sitting next to me was a young man I did not know. He was gazing into the distance where a deep valley stretched before us. A wide river was meandering along it. It was a lovely restful scene.

This chap knew my name it seems. He knew more than that because he had spent a long time with me in my life. He had been trying to help me along - not always there, but quite often. He had passed ideas to me when he felt I needed a bit of inspiration. I must say I had never felt any kind of outside help coming through. I was never interested in this sort of thing.

I would never discuss it with my father, who had been sensitive all of his life. Really, I had felt a bit ashamed of my dad and his being a medium. When I was younger, the lads around used to pull my leg - that is until Dad did some healing on one of the neighbourhood dogs that had got run over and was almost dead. We were all there at the time - we had seen the actual accident and felt the shock and the helplessness. So when my dad came along and just laid his hands along the dog's body, we all felt some kind of relief that someone was doing something. I remember that we all crouched round him, waiting for a miracle - and it happened. The dog eventually wagged it's tail and moved its head to lick my dad's hand!

After that I never got teased - in fact I seemed to be more popular and always people brought their animals to our house for Dad to heal.

All of this had flashed through my mind as I was sitting there looking into the valley. I remembered how I had put the whole thing completely out of my mind when I had grown up and gone into the Airforce.

Then, later on, the subject was rarely mentioned for I was out of the house a lot when I had met Mary and then I had got married, and Dad's doings didn't really come into my life again. He never ever forced his ideas on anyone.

What happens now I wondered. Immediately, it seemed, my new found friend told me it was up to me what I did. There were a lot of people I could go along and meet - people I would feel quite at home with.

'How can I,' I thought, 'when I haven't even met them yet?'

'Do you feel comfortable with me?' he asked.

I had to admit that I did. He only spoke when I asked him or wondered anything. He didn't push himself on to me.

So off we went - walking along down into a largish village - very pleasant, and to a big house with nice grounds and lots of young people about. They were all talking and laughing and the atmosphere was very pleasant. They all seemed to nod or smile as we passed and then I was introduced to a couple who seemed as though they might own the place. Again I liked them and they offered me a drink - just like a cocktail party, and we sat down to talk.

The interesting thing about it was that they offered me a job!

They seemed to know I had been involved with personnel all my life and I was just what they needed it seemed, to help a few people with settling in problems. I suggested that I, too had a few problems in that direction, but they seemed to think those would disappear as I helped the others.

So, that's what I did and what I still do. As they said, it was my forte and I soon began to feel at home.

All that I have told you now - about how I died in a crush at a football match, I had really almost forgotten! When I was approached to contribute my experience for this book, I had to sit down and bring it all back to my mind - just like you do now when you look at old photos. You seem to relive it all again, don't you? The strange thing is, though, when I relived my death, I realised that although it sounds horrifying, to be crushed to death, I can't for the life of me (if you'll excuse the expression!) remember feeling other than the initial bits I have described to you. They didn't last long either!

I suppose the conclusion that can be drawn from my story, is that things look worse to the watcher than they are to the victim. So try never to imagine what might be - because you are most likely to be wrong, and you will only be wasting your emotions, your sympathies and your energies.

BERTHE

We were waiting at the barrier, for the little ferry that took people from island to island. It was not a large boat, it carried about sixty passengers and a couple of cars. The men who manned the ferry had been at sea most of their lives, and this job was really prior to their retirement - they were all in their late fifties, with the exception of a lad to do the more energetic jobs.

The wind was getting up and seeing as it was blowing off the land, we would no doubt have a speedier crossing. It was quite dark, but that made no difference to the crew. They must have known this stretch of water like the back of their hands.

The wind was seemingly making it hard work to get in, for the ferry was now running about ten minutes late. At last, someone at the front of the queue, near the barrier, saw the lights and announced it to everyone else. We all shuffled a bit, as it was cold standing here in the wind.

The boat landed and was tied up and passengers disembarked followed by a car and some packages and a couple of sheep.

Then our queue started moving and we were soon aboard - everyone going down into the saloon, where they could sit at little tables, like a school canteen, and have a cup of coffee or tea from a wax cup, if they so desired.

Jan and I sat down but we did not want a drink. It was a bit tightly packed but we all cheerfully closed up to make room for others. There was certainly a crowd this evening - no doubt there was something going on on the mainland.

For the most part people were not talking much, but I did happen to hear one thin-faced lady tell her companion, she had seen them bringing a coffin on board at the last minute. Her face showed her dislike at such an occurrence and I began thinking of those on the island who died, who either belonged to the mainland, or who had wished to be buried on the mainland. Some of the islands were so small that no-one was allowed to be buried on them.

At last it seemed we were off. All of the banging and shouting was over and in the relative quiet, all that could be heard was the chugging of the engines, the wind pushing us away from the jetty and the gurgling of the water as the boat cut her way across its surface.

The lamps hanging in the saloon were the old-fashioned oil lamps. They cast a soft but patchy light, except where the coffee and tea were dispensed. This was only a long counter with enough room for one person behind it to make the drinks, but above his head there were four lamps hanging and the area was very bright.

People began to chat quietly amongst themselves and soon their steady drone added to the sounds of the boat. It was choppy, I must say. Those with drinks had to drink them off quickly or they would be spilt over tables and clothes. There were a few people standing, and they were obliged to hang on to whatever they had near them, as it would have been difficult to stand otherwise.

We had been moving along at a seeming fast but not at all smooth pace, for about ten minutes, when a gust of wind swung the little boat around and we all felt the movement and the sudden dropping down as if the sea had opened up a hole. Talk was suspended and we all seemed to wait for the boat to come up again. Shouts from above alerted us to the fact that we were not going up. The ferry overturned.

After that first realisation, there was no time for any kind of action. We were all thrown as one body crashing to what would have been the ceiling of the saloon. There were screams which became muffled with the mass of bodies - and that was all I remembered.

I opened my eyes out of a dream which was quite unpleasant. I dreamt I had been in a boat which had been over-turned in a rough sea. I would have been drowned if I hadn't woken myself up. What a relief! Jan was beside me and asleep, so I decided to get up and make us a coffee. I got a shock.

We were not in our apartment in Rotterdam. We were in some kind of hospital, with rooms all along one side and a huge glass window along the other. The view out of the window was really marvellous! Rolling hills, a river sparkling in the distance, a blue, blue sky - it was all fresh and lovely. As I turned from the window, Jan had come and stood alongside of me.

'Where are we?' I asked him. 'I can't understand what is happening, can you?'

Jan took a hold of my shoulders quite gently - 'No, I am not at all sure of where we are, but there is something I am very sure of!'

His voice sounded a little strange - a little excitable, I thought.

'We have died!' he said. He looked hard at me to see how I would take it.

'Don't be silly, how can we be dead? You are solid and so am I. We are not ghosts are we?'

'You must remember we were on the little ferry return-ing to the mainland from our holiday?'

It was then that I felt my heart lurch - well it was as if my heart had lurched - the feeling was. Then I had NOT been dreaming! I told Jan that I thought that was all a dream I had been having.

'No, that was real. I think everyone would have drowned - the sea was so rough out of the harbour - they were

16

turning the boat from what I could gather, and she got caught in a squall and over she went.'

'How could you gather any of that when we were sitting very closely packed together in the saloon? How could you have talked to any of the crew?'

Jan looked at me and swallowed. 'It was very strange, Berthe. As the boat went over and everyone was hurtled down, I seemed to be outside of myself, watching the whole thing. I was even able to be with the crew as well, as they struggled to get a lifeboat. They made the attempt but they had no time. Then I seemed to be above the sea and I saw the waves close over the boat. It was uncanny! I didn't panic at all. I felt quite calm and detached about it all. Then I looked for you and found you with your body. I got a hold of your hand and said 'Come on, Berthe' and you came. I noticed other people, too, just leaving their bodies. Some wouldn't, they stayed with the boat. I tried to tell them all to come. I didn't know where, but we seemed to go up through a dark avenue of trees and just as we were coming into the light, I went unconscious. Curious that was, like delayed shock or something. Then I woke up to see you looking out of the window.'

'Well, where are we? Can we really be dead, Jan? Why are we still solid? This can't be Heaven can it - even though that view is heavenly - it is not what I expect Heaven to be like.'

'I don't know about anything really. I think we should have a look round and try to find someone to ask.'

At that moment, a man was coming towards us along the corridor. He was smiling and as he approached, I realised it was my father! My father had been dead for the past ten years at least!

'Yes, it is me, Berthe,' he said and he shook hands with Jan.'I am a little late in coming to meet you. Things don't change, do they? At least I don't, I was always in trouble with your mother for being late!'

I had to smile at this because it was my mother's constant complaint - Father's inability to be punctual. 'Absent-minded Professor' we had all called him. He was a professor -

of History. Then I thought again about our situation.

'Father, are we dead?'

'I am afraid you are, dear. The ferry turned turtle and went down. No-one suffered. Everyone has been taken care of - apart from the corpse, of course!'

I immediately thought of the thin-faced woman being anxious because of the coffin on board.

'Yes, she proved to be a little difficult to help, that lady - superstitious about so many things, I'm afraid,' my father said.

'How did you know what I was thinking about?' I asked.

'That is how we communicate - by thought. Now come along, I have a nice house and we can go there and have a really good talk about everything - I will try to answer every one of your questions.'

That is what we did. I was, and still am, very, very amazed at all that has happened to us. I am finding out more each moment of my life - yes MY LIFE. I feel more alive here than I felt there in your world. Things are very different and I need to go gently and not ask too many questions. Jan is far quicker than I and often goes off investigating all sorts of things. I have made a few friends who are like me, a little slower and happier to take things steadily.

One thing I have been very impressed with is just how much my old life, as I call it, affects this, my new life. I regret a lot of things. I regret allowing myself to be led along with the crowd instead of doing what I REALLY wanted to follow myself, in my very own way. I allowed people's opinions to influence me far more than I should - I have found out that it does not really matter if others think you odd or different because you are not like them.

I always wanted to be liked and approved of and I have found out that I was wrong to be like that. Oh, there are so many things I could tell you, but I will not. I will just say that I really did not know that I had died and it came as a very pleasant surprise to me.

PHILIP

I loved my job. I was a fireman working for the railway. I know a lot of kids used to dream of being an engine driver, but I always wanted to be a fireman. I liked the manual effort of first filling up the coal tender. We always had to load our own coal, and I preferred that. I was one of those people who always liked to do the whole job themselves.

I used to feel very good swinging my great shovel full of coal from the heap to the truck. I know I always had a little smile on my face because I was very fit - I used to do weight training twice a week, to keep fit. Really I don't know if I did it to keep fit for the job!

I worked with Bert. He was a good driver and we were a good team. We were together for ten years.

I was a married man. I had got married when I was quite young- too young, really. I had met Madge at the local swimming baths. Most of the youngsters of the district went swimming at least once a week. I never went dancing, though. I was a bit more serious, I suppose than the rest of the lads. I was more of a loner.

There was a weight-training club near us, but I liked to do all of my training on my own. I used to see a few of the club lads at the swimming baths, strutting around and rarely having a swim! They didn't realise, I'm sure just how good swimming was for developing muscles and keeping you fit. They seemed to like parading around the sides of the open-air pool like a load of turkey cocks!

Anyway I got married and soon we had a couple of kids - a boy and a girl. Nice enough kids, but I was not really a family man. I liked work and tended to do as much overtime as I could.

You have no idea how good it was to get your fire stoked up and feel the pull of the engine and the rest of the train. I tried to keep our pull as smooth as possible, which meant not allowing the fire to get too low before stoking it up again.

19

It is an art, I think, being a fireman and keeping your speed steady. What a lovely sound - the hissing of the steam and the clicking of the wheels along the tracks!

Bert was quite as serious about his job as I was about mine. This is why we made a good team I suppose. We worked long hours, Bert and me - sometimes clocking up 50 hours a week. The money was good of course, but we liked the job. There was something exciting about travelling around - even when you were on a local run every day, going to the same places and back. A few of the drivers used to race each other on the routine jobs - just to break the monotony I suppose. Bert and I never joined in this childish pastime though.

We didn't talk a lot when you consider the number of hours we spent working together each day. Our conversation was mainly about the engine, the rest of the train, the tracks, the quality of the coal. Sometimes we looked at the countryside around us on a long run. Like me, Bert lived for his job.

One day, as I was clocking on for work, I was called into the office and told the boss wanted to talk to me. I hadn't a lot of time, and when I was called into his office, I asked if it was going to take long, as I wanted to get loaded.

'I'm putting Len Green on with Bert today,' the boss said.

I just stared at him in disbelief.

'I want you to train a lad,' he went on.

'Train a lad!' I repeated. I had never trained anyone in my life.

'Aye. I've a young lad who could do all right stoking but I want him training well, and I think you're the man for the job. Come on I'll take you to him and we'll get you both started.'

'Just a minute Mr.Garvy. I don't think I can do it. I've no experience.'

'All you have to do is show him how you do the job yourself - from beginning to end. George Brenshaw is standing in sidings with 7631 and when you're ready, he'll follow your instructions. Don't worry - you can do it, you're one of the best there is at the job.'

Well, to cut a long story short, I had to train this lad up. I must admit I wasn't happy - first because I didn't like my pattern changing, and second because I didn't want to give away all my tricks of the trade. It took three weeks for him to get the main idea of the job and then I went off to the boss to see when I could get back to Bert and our teamwork.

'You'll have to team up with Harry Flocks this week. Bert is on his holidays. You'll be on the London run, though, so you should be happy.'

I wasn't happy, I'm afraid, because Harry was one of the main racing drivers - he was as childish as they come, and I was not keen on having to do things his way. Still. I had no choice - the boss was the boss.

It was along the High Embankment that we left the rails. I had my head down stoking away and I had no idea Harry had run a signal way back before we entered the valley run up. It was a signal which requested the driver to observe a speed limit to enable a local stopping train to get through this valley, along the embankment, before we started on it. I think he must have misjudged the speed of the train in front, because he was on top of it before he realised he couldn't stop in time. I heard a tremendous crash, felt the engine judder and then nothing.

When I came to, I was in agony. My head and shoulders were agonisingly painful. Then I blacked out and it seems that on the way to the hospital, I died. You might say I died by my own hands because my upper body was almost burnt to a cinder as the great engine toppled over, and the fires I was stoking rushed out on to me.

The oddest thing though was that after a very long time sleeping or unconscious - call it what you will, I woke up. No burns. No injuries. But strangest of all, I could not contact in any way, the world I had lived in. I was a ghost in other words.

I found out I needed no food or drink or sustenance of any kind. I discovered after a time that I could move around at a very fast pace - in fact I only needed to think of a place or person and I was there.

I then spent a very long time (although I could not have

told anyone just how long, as I could not keep track of the time really) riding with the engines up and down the country. It was a wonderful experience to begin with. I was there first with Bert and his new fireman - the lad I, myself had trained. I am proud to say, that this lad became a very good fireman and I heard Bert tell him that he was almost, but not quite as good as I had been.

When Bert said this, I was quite shocked by the strength of his feelings. He almost went to pieces and I had to help him get his mind back on the job. He was passing a big signal box at the time, with a very complicated set of signals that needed concentration. Still I didn't realise that in his way, old Bert felt very deep feelings of brotherly love for me. It took him a long time in fact to get over my death. I used to ride mostly with him, but when he was off, I rode with other drivers - even the continental drivers that I was able to pick up from time to time.

Bert's health was never quite the same after the shock of my death, so he was off sick quite a lot. One day when I was riding with him, I realised he was getting past it. He had missed a few signals and I managed to jog his memory to save any problems. After the last run, when he went to clock off, the boss was just coming out of his office. Bert asked to see him. To my amazement Bert asked to be signed off for good - due to his ill-health.

Well it happened and after that I didn't really have a lot of heart for the trains.

I was mooching about when a chap approached me and actually spoke to me. I was quite amazed for no-one had ever spoken to me, since I died. I had spent a lot of time with my wife and family, since I became a 'ghost' I suppose you could say, but not one of them knew I was there or tried to speak to me. They like most bereaved families, grieved and gradually adjusted to life without me. It wasn't too difficult as I had spent a lot of my time at work and on overtime and none of them really knew me.

So, when this chap asked me did I know the date, I was taken aback. He looked quite an ordinary fellow, quietly dressed, about my age I suppose.

'What do you mean?' I asked him.

'Do you realise that you've been haunting engines for five years?' he said.

Well you could have knocked me down with a feather - five years!

'The thing is,' the young chap went on, 'there is a lot of work needs doing and we're a bit short-handed. You've always been a good worker, and you've a cool head in spite of working so close to fire, so I wondered if you'd give us a hand.'

'What sort of work are you talking about?' I asked, as cautious as ever.

'Nothing really difficult. You know how you trained up that young lad as a fireman and did a really good job of it?' he looked at me as my mouth had fallen open.

'How the devil did you know that?' I asked.

'I've been keeping an eye on you - ready for this moment really. I know quite a bit about you because, as you've been haunting the engines all over the place, so have I been haunting you. Only it is not really haunting, you know. You come under the group of people- and it is a very big group - who are earthbound. That means you are staying around your old habit patterns and so you are getting nowhere but bored.'

I thought how right he was with this last bit, but the rest of it puzzled me.

'Don't worry about what I say, just come along and see what our problem is.'

Well I felt a bit of a fool because he suddenly took a hold of my hand and said 'Hold on!'

There was a blur all around me and I know I was travelling because I had discovered how to do this since I had died, but I seemed to be going at quite a rate!

Then we stopped. It was very early morning - must have been winter because there was some kind of feeling to the air. We were quite close to a big block of flats, probably on the Continent, as we didn't have such huge blocks in England. Suddenly there was a roar and a wall of flame shot up into the air. Now the odd thing about this was that although I could see the flames and hear all of the crackling and screams, I didn't feel any heat and the flame didn't seem to touch us.

'Come on, follow me!' my new friend said.

We dived right into it all and soon I could see bodies all around me - but the strangest thing was that there seemed to be twins of everyone. One was the real body, burning or just lying out of the flames but overcome by the fumes and smoke, and hovering near the bodies were identical bodies, looking scared and not really knowing what to do.

I immediately went for a couple of kids that were clinging together. I put my arms around them both and said 'Come on, you're all right, I'll take you away.'

Then I just thought of a hospital and in no time we were there, all three of us. As soon as I had put them down, a couple of nurses came along and took them over.

'Go back' one of them said smiling at me.

I again thought of the fire and I was there again, bringing out more people. This went on for a long time. Each time at the hospital, there was always an air of calm and efficiency. The people I had taken in were no longer in sight when I brought the others - no doubt taken very good care of by the nurses.

Eventually the fire was put out. It must have taken a couple of days from what I could gather from the Fire Chief talking to the police. When I had deposited my last patient, a youngish woman, quite attractive, I thought, with a very lovely smile despite the horror she had just experienced, I turned at a familiar voice alongside of me.

It was my friend again, and he was smiling at me.

'You see what I mean, when I said we needed you? You have been a tremendous help to me. Thank you. I'm glad I was right about you!'

'What do you mean? You seem to make a lot of remarks that I can't fathom!' I smiled at him because I liked him and felt we were on the same wavelength. That was strange for me as I had never really made friends easily.

'Well we have a little team that specialises in helping out where fire is concerned - when people are killed and need help. Just as you have been doing. It seemed like second nature to you, didn't it?' he said.

'Well, I must say I found it interesting to be able to get people out, comfort them and get them to a hospital. Are you offering me a job then? I thought you only worked in the physical earth life - not when you become a ghost!'

'Well, as you know yourself, you can choose what you do. You can hang about haunting the old places, but nobody can see or hear you and it does get a bit boring. You can go off and make a few friends, get yourself fixed up with a place to live and then perhaps look at a few new ideas to develop yourself - or you can help us. You can still look around as well - see what else there is on offer. There is always plenty to do. You will never ever be bored. What do you say to sticking with us? I will take you to meet the rest of the team if you are interested......oh, and we might be able to use that young lady you brought out last, as soon as she is feeling better!'

So that is what I now do with my time. I also have developed an interest - don't laugh! - in painting! I study with people who were once quite known on the earth - the main thing is they certainly can teach a thing or two about colour and texture.

Brigitte, the lady I brought out last, is working with us in the rescue team and she is also studying - music. We are quite inseparable apart from our studies. She is the opposite of myself in many ways, and we have some very interesting discussions!

DOROTHY

Everything was dark around me. I couldn't see a thing. It was a strange feeling - the silence and the darkness. I didn't feel frightened at all, I was just waiting for something, I think. I was probably waiting for someone to put a light on.

Then my mind started thinking of things, the usual things, plans for the next day; conversations I had had recently;

my job and the people at work; and I thought about what I was hoping to buy next. There were a few worries about my inability to make long-term relationships with guys. It was funny really, I was mad keen on them for a while and then I started finding fault with them in some way and the relationship began to break up.

Was it myself being too choosy? I know I soon got bored in lots of ways with things. Short-term - that's what I liked best. Short trips with my family here and there, shopping expeditions and that sort of thing. Anything lasting a bit longer, and we were soon at loggerheads and bawling at each other. I know that happens in most families according to my friends.

I wonder what I really want in life? Even my jobs didn't last long - certainly not long enough for me to get promoted - but then I don't think I wanted promotion and the responsibility that brought. I felt that I didn't want ever to be too tied down to anything.

My friends talked a lot about getting married and having babies and a nice house somewhere. Ugh! I didn't fancy that one little bit. No sir! I couldn't imagine anything worse. I didn't like babies or kids, anyway. My family always seemed anxious that I should be settling down - I think they feel I am a bit late at twenty nine - an old maid in fact! I know I am not at all old in myself and I don't feel that I look old either.

Sometimes I think they envy me being free to go off when I like on trips - just like............oh! it's getting lighter! Where on earth am I? Good Heavens it's a hospital, a kid's hospital and I am walking up to the front doors. Just as I am about to open the doors, they open and a young intern comes out - at least he looks like an intern, with a white jacket.

'Oh, excuse me, are you the new help?'

He certainly has a nice smile. 'No, I'm just a visitor.'

'Oh.' He looked disappointed for a moment. 'Well do you think you can give me a hand with a case who is due to arrive any minute?'

'Well, I'm not a nurse - I'm not qualified in any way medically. I can't really be of help to you, I'm afraid,' I replied.

'You don't need medical qualifications, you just need to

have some love in you and surely you have that?' He looked straight at me. It was quite embarrassing.

'Yeah, sure. I'll help all I can' I managed to get out.

He smiled immediately, 'Good, just come with me will you?'

We turned a corner of the building and entered another door into a very pretty room - it seemed to be done out in pastel colours and there was a lovely glow about it and a very nice feeling.

'Will you just sit there on that seat,' and he waved me to a seat at one side of the room. To my amazement he sat down opposite me against the other side of the room. Then my stomach lurched for, in between us, in the middle of the room, there appeared a huge screen and on the screen was a picture of a very small boy riding a seemingly new bike along a track. At the bottom of the track, the gate was open and he rode straight out into the path of an automobile. It was so instant - a scream of brakes, the automobile swerved to avoid the bike, but it was no use at all. The small body lay motionless in the dust. Then, to my amazement, he seemed to get up and totter off quite unconcerned and, to my surprise, I saw the young doctor opposite me walking towards the boy. I felt myself rise too and almost run to the kid and I reached him first and swept him up in my arms, holding him close to me.

The screen and the scene disappeared and there we were in the pretty room, myself holding the boy and the doctor holding a bike - an exact replica of the one we had just seen bent out of all recognition.

'Come on. Joe, get on your bike, and this time be careful where you are going!'

The kid seemed a little puzzled and looked from me to the doctor and the bike, and then made as if to get down, so I put him on the floor so that he could go to the bike.

I got the idea the doctor had told me it was important that Joe got back on his bike - to remove any fear he might have incurred. It wasn't that he actually spoke the words - I just seemed to know.

With the doctor bending and holding on to Joe's shoulder as he pedalled, we moved out of the room into what looked like a play yard, almost full of kids of all ages. There seemed to be plenty of room though, because most of them were involved in some kind of activity. Joe was let free to ride quite happily amongst the others and we sat down on a convenient seat, where we could watch all that went on. It sure was a strange place and I was beginning to worry about where it all was - myself included!

'My name's John,' my doctor friend said. 'What do you think to this place of ours?'

'Well, I was just thinking, I have never in my life seen such a hospital. These kids all seem fit and from what we just saw back there - how come little Joe is in one piece?'

'His soul is in one piece. What we saw back there, was his body being rendered useless in the accident.'

I stared at the guy with my mouth wide open I am afraid! I just could not believe this take on at all.

'You just have to be kidding here, John! I really cannot grasp what is happening but you are not making sense. I am beginning to feel a bit weird and in need of a doctor myself, I think!'

'Hold on. You're O.K. Just listen a while if you will.'

Then he began to talk at length, and at the same time the sun came out and a beautiful glow bathed the seat where we sat. I felt the warmth - and happiness even that the sun always brought out in me. I refocussed on John. He was reminding me of a trip I took, out to Hawaii. This was my annual holidays and on them I had gone with a small group on a motor boat to see some outlying small islands. We had had a nice day, exploring the islands, we had swum around a little and I had decided to scuba to get a look at the fish and sea life down there. As John spoke, I felt myself becoming a little dizzy. My head began to spin and I couldn't breathe. I started to struggle for breath and then felt one almighty pain in my chest - then nothing. Then blackness.

Then I was there sitting on the seat by John, the sun warm on me, feeling good. I knew what had happened to me. I had caught my airline on a sharp rock whilst exploring a small cave near the bottom of the sea bed. It must have fractured and in my struggle to get out of the cave I caught my head on the rocky roof.

'So then what happened?' I asked my companion.

He looked at me, holding my eyes. 'You died.'

For a long moment I sat there unable to speak. It was too much to take in really. I needed to get my thoughts straight.

Then I said 'What is this place?'

'It's a kind of hospital or reception for some who die. You saw Joe's accident - you helped him over. It serves a purpose, and that's why it is here.'

The mention of Joe caused thoughts in my mind. 'What will happen to him and the other kids?'

'We have to gently bring them to a realisation that they have died. As yet for some of them there is no such word - or meaning, in their minds. We also have to help them adjust to the change in their homes and parents. Fortunately kids, if given love, will soon respond. They are very adaptable.'

'Who will give them that love?' I asked.

'People like yourself.'

I went into another long silence at that. John was a very strange guy. I had never met anyone quite like him. He somehow seemed to induce feelings within me and at the same time he seemed to put down other feelings which might well have caused me to panic.

'It is not just me helping you this way. There are quite a lot of friends around you, some of whom I am sure you have knowledge.'

I suddenly had a picture of a scene when I had gone North on a skiing trip. In my usual headstrong way, I had got up very early one morning because I wanted to ski the fresh snow on the main slope. It was a high and difficult run, but I was a competent skier, I thought, and it would present quite a bit of excitement to me. The stupid thing about the whole scheme was that it was a rule of the Ski Club, that no one person went up alone. It was of course a safety rule and as such made sense. But......when did I go for sense in my life?

Well I told the guy on the chair lift I was meeting some

friends from round the other side, so he let me go up. It was really beautiful up there. Down below me stretched the dazzling virgin snow. The run I was skiing, was bending and winding down, with a few belts of trees to circle and a few nice humps to jump. Looking at it, my mouth watered, and off I went.

It was wonderful until I turned into the right channel and circled a thick wood on the edge of a hill. As I came round, I realised I was in a huge drift of soft snow and below me was surely a very deep hollow - I could only go down!

My reflex action was to close my eyes. That's all I could have done, there was no way out of that mess. But somehow I got the feeling of flying as on a jump. I opened my eyes and could see below and ahead of me the sloping side of the hill. Another six feet and I would be on firm ground again. Alongside of me was another skier. This person was all in red - so not a club instructor. We landed absolutely together but my companion stayed just behind me. I felt rather than saw him or her. When I finally got down, breathless yet stimulated, I turned to the other skier as I pushed up my goggles. I was completely alone. There was no-one else there - but I did have a very strong feeling that someone had said in my ear, very distinctly, 'Your ninth life!'

Later on, I decided that the excitement of the near-disaster had caused me to imagine things. I must have even imagined the snow drift - or how could I have got over it?

Now, as I sat here with John, I knew - knew without doubt, that someone HAD been with me. Not only then, because I had been quite reckless all my life. I had had a few near misses. Someone must have been keeping an eye on me, and bailing me out of the messes I got myself in.

'So, what happens now?' I asked.

'Maybe you will eventually be able to develop another side of yourself - your soft, motherly, passive nature. Maybe, now and again you can come over here to this place and help a few kids to have a soft landing - like you did Joe. Maybe all manner of things......' John smiled at me and I think that for once I really understood what he meant.

ERIC

Isn't it funny how your life changes? Mine did, and I'll tell you all about the biggest change anyone can ever have in their life.

There were five men sitting around a table. I say men but I was not much more than a lad, I suppose. I was twenty. We were all in Her Majesty's Navy, being paid to see the world.

I loved travelling and this was certainly a good way of being on the move - in more ways than one. Her Majesty's ships were sailing ships. I was just a rating, I hadn't done much to get up the ladder - I wasn't one for heights. I did everything that was called for, or that I was ordered to do. I didn't mind taking orders - the officers weren't so bad.

The food was good, I must say. There were a lot of rumours before I took the Queen's shilling, that the food was poor and many sailors suffered scurvy and other skin problems, but I didn't find that to be true. Our meals were good and varied and nourishing and I, for one had no complaints. I'm sure that the fish hadn't either when Cook threw the remains and scraps over the back of the ship!

After the meal that I was telling you about, I went off to my post that day, on top of the mast. There were a few jobs to do up there - jobs I had done many a time before and going up the mast was no problem.

I hadn't been up there very long when a sharp wind got up. It was a sudden, brisk wind that seemed to chop and change direction and of course the sea did the same. It was whipped up and the waves were big. I checked the top rigging and made sure that nothing was flapping that shouldn't have been flapping, and I just turned a fraction and moved my foot a little and before I knew it, I was falling off the mast!

As I fell, face up fortunately, many thoughts seemed to come into my mind. Not in a great rush though. I wondered first about my Mam in Sheffield. How would she take the news? What would she do with my things? Then I wondered if I'd hit the deck or the sea. As I had gone over backwards and the ship was rolling about like a drunk on a Saturday night, it was not guaranteed that I would hit the deck. Isn't it funny, at a time like that to be wondering such things?

Well, so far as I was concerned, I never did hit the deck. My body did but I had no recollection of it doing so. What happened you might ask. Well I just never stopped all of the thoughts going through my mind about what would happen if.....

These thoughts just went on and on and became quite involved because every now and then I would go off at a tangent. For example, I wondered what my cousin would say. She had not wanted me to join the Navy. She might have been a bit 'knowledgeable' as they used to say. She might have had some idea I would end up falling off the mast! However, as I thought of how she would take the news that I had, I then went off and wondered if she and her husband were happy in their extremely 'fast off the mark' marriage. I had just heard from my mother that this cousin had got married and that no-one had known that she was even courting!

Then my mind went back to when we were all small together. How we used to have our little gangs and fall in and out of friends with each gang on a very regular basis. It was all very ordinary thinking, like everyone does almost all of their life.

I suppose because I was thinking so much of home, It was no real shock when I found myself walking along the street of small houses to where we lived. My mother was out but I went in and sat myself down in the chair I used to use when home, opposite that of my mother. By the fire it was.

Eventually my mother came home, made herself a cup of tea, after putting her shopping away, and sat down opposite me. I smiled at her. She didn't know I was there because she couldn't see me of course.

I wondered just how I was going to tell her that I had fallen off the mast and was now dead. Isn't it funny how I knew that I was dead myself and yet there I was at home, trying to bridge the gap between the living and the so-called dead?

As I sat there very comfortable in the chair, I tried hard to think how to tell her I was there. As I did so, she suddenly put her cup down with a clatter.

'Something's happened to our Eric!' she said to herself. I could hear just what she said somehow, so there must be some bridge between us.

My mother turned quite white and as she looked ill to me, I got up and knelt down by her and took her hands. I was glad to see the colour came back to her face, but instead I was taken aback to see great tears falling down her cheeks! Isn't it funny how some people - especially the womenfolk, can cry for no reason? My mother didn't know for sure that I was dead, but here she was crying already!

I decided that I would stay with her so I would be there when the news came. Seeing as I was there, I decided I would go upstairs to my bed and get a bit of sleep. I had been working long hours recently, and had not had much sleep. That might well have been why I missed my footing on the top of the mast. Anyway I went to sleep as soon as my head touched the pillow it seemed!

I was woken up by a feeling of apprehension. Something was about to happen and so I got up and went downstairs. It was morning - about six o'clock I should think, listening to the chiming clock in the corner. There was a great thudding on the door and my mother came downstairs in her dressing gown. I went with her to the front door. It was a telegraph boy and he gave my mother the envelope and waited to see if she wanted to send any reply.

I put my arms around my mother as she read the news. The boy went off on his bike and I helped mother to her chair. I really wanted to make her a cup of tea, but I knew I wasn't really able to handle things at all. I had worked it out - I could only send ideas. I sent the idea very strongly to Mrs. Green, who lived next door, and was really glad about Mrs. Green's habit of peering through her net curtains every time somebody knocked on my mother's door! Isn't it funny how such a habit could one day turn out to be useful?

Anyway, I left my mother with Mrs Green and a big pot of tea.

The reason I left them was that I couldn't do any more - and also because I had a strong feeling I should be somewhere else. Into my mind came a picture of a nice beach, with a palm tree and the sun shining down - and before you could say 'Isn't it funny?' that is exactly where I found myself. I stretched out on the sand in the sun and went to sleep. I felt that life would sort itself out eventually.

GWEN

It was a lovely day and I walked happily with the children along Common Lane. Robert was kicking his ball along the grass verge and I was a bit anxious it might either go on to the road or into the ditch, so I stooped and picked it up, as it came alongside of me. Robert did not see me pick up the ball and thought he had lost it. He shouted out 'Stop everybody! Lost me ball!' Jemmy and I stopped and turned back towards him and that's when it happened.

From out of nowhere, it seemed, a van came hurtling on to the verge at speed, and my last memory is of Robert being thrown up into the air like a doll, his arms and legs spread eagled out grotesquely. That was the pain - and the only pain I knew, then blankness - total quiet, safe nothing.

It was a journey we made every day - down to the village, to the shop and post office, to post Bill's letters. This time, however we didn't get there and Bill didn't get his letters from me and the children.

My next consciousness was of Bill. He was straggling a small wall, holding a tape measure reel, whilst his colleague at the other side of the flat piece of scrub land, marked the position he wanted with an iron rod, hammered into the ground. I watched as the man tied a piece of cloth on to the rod. He had written five hundred and seventy on the cloth. It was strange that I knew what he had written because I couldn't see the numbers - I was standing behind Bill, waiting for him to turn round and see me.

As I focussed again on my husband, he half turned towards me, a puzzled look on his face. He held up his arm and looked at his watch. It was eleven o'clock in the morning, in the desert, that he had worked in for the past two years. This was his last job, and he thought of it as I stared at him.

He didn't see me - he couldn't because I really wasn't there. With my son, Robert, I had been killed by a bread van, out of control in a country lane. My daughter, Jemmy had only been caught a blow to the side of her head, and she fell clear of the wheels of the vehicle. She had been unconscious for almost an hour and then had been checked by the hospital doctor, but had only bruising. I had stayed with her at the hospital. She didn't know though, as she slept most of the time - even when she regained consciousness, she slipped back into a sleep.

'It will help her forget the accident,' the young doctor said.

I don't know what happened to Robert. I just did not see him at all. This is why I thought of my husband, because I couldn't find Robert. Some part of my muddled mind thought he might be with Bill.

Suddenly Bill called out to his colleague 'I want to go to the phone, Geoff. I'll get one of the boys to help you here.' He then strode off to where there were some low single storey buildings on wheels. Portable offices and such that Bill's firm took everywhere they went in the world, as they built the new factories.

I was with Bill when he telephoned our house. I was also somehow at the house as well and was able to see my mother, very pale and shaky as she picked up the phone. Bill asked if everything was all right. My mother almost fainted as she heard his voice. All had been done that she had to do. A cable had been sent out to the agents - only a short time ago - too short for Bill to have heard the awful news. I knew my mother was going to find it hard to tell Bill personally, and so I went up to her to try to give her strength. I knew already that I couldn't touch her - I had tried to take Jemmy in my arms and found it impossible. However I knew I could get closer than touching and so I enveloped my mother with as much love as I could - strength and love, just as she used to do for me when I was a girl. I formed the words for her in my mind and then I heard her repeating them - it was uncanny because it sounded just like me! Then I focussed on Bill again and enveloped him in my love - just as well because he almost dropped the phone and his tanned face lightened with the shock. Even though he had had some idea all was not well - it must always be a shock for anyone. I certainly did not expect Bill to faint! But he did. Just went down as if he had been pole axed.

Then everything went black for me again.

I dreamed this time. In my dream, I was walking into a kind of Disneyland with Robert holding tightly on to my hand. I didn't have to bend down to look at his face, but I knew just what his expression was. He couldn't believe it! His little hand clutched at mine as he looked from side to side and tried to make his mind up which he wanted to try first.

Just like him, he decided on a little train that seemed to go all the way round the place, up hill, down dale and through tunnels. We both got on, I was surprised just how much room there was for me, I had expected to be cramped being so tall. What a ride we had! The tunnels were not dark but on the contrary filled with the prettiest lights and scenes of animals in their natural state, looking very life-like. It was a lovely ride for me, never mind Robert. His eyes were everywhere and he shouted with his usual enthusiasm that I hadn't the heart to curb.

When we finally got off at a little station - it was a miniature real-life place with everything that old railway stations used to have, I remember. There were porters and barrows, tubs of flowers and a station master. Then, as we went through the turnstile, Robert saw a big lake with little motor boats on it and he pulled me along for our next experience.

Robert and I spent a long time in that world of fun and adventure. We were not at all aware of time or anything else. There were of course other people having fun and we smiled at them from time to time, if they seemed our kind of people. Then, as we were walking along a pretty path of all coloured, sparkling, smooth stone, we almost bumped into another boy of Robert's age, who was being pulled along by a huge St.Bernard's dog - a real, full-sized Nanna! Robert immediately stopped and talked to the boy and the dog, and somehow we joined up and became a little group on our own.

Robert soon was holding the lead of the dog, and his little friend was having a ride on its back. We came to a beautiful meadow and decided to sit down for a rest. I say a rest, but I didn't feel at all tired, which was strange because Robert had so much energy, he usually soon tired me out with his games.

I stretched out on the soft grass, and, when a young female asked if she might join me, I was glad of her company. I thought she was Rod's mother - Rod was Robert's new friend. No, she was just looking after him. It seemed that Rod had been knocked down and killed, whilst running across a road near his home. His mother hadn't been there at the time, for Rod was allowed to play out with his friends, whilst she got on with her housework or had friends in for a coffee.

Julie had been there when Rod died, she immediately became his surrogate mother. She had a lovely personality. She said she tried not to crowd Rod, for he had become very independent, because of his mother's tendency to leave him to play on his own. Julie was always there with him but was able to be invisible, in some way. I was interested in this and determined I would find out about it more, when I got the chance.

Julie laughed at me and said 'It's no good thinking things, you know - you might as well say them. Thoughts can't be kept to yourself here! If you want to be private or even invisible, you just have to put yourself on to a different wavelength.'

Well, we talked about this and she helped me achieve it. It was all a matter of focussing and not focussing. I became quite good and felt a bit like the cat in Alice in Wonderland appearing and disappearing. Eventually Robert noticed something was going on and wanted to be in on it. Of course he was a bit young yet so we fobbed him off.

I decided to confide in Julie about my other worries - Jemmy and Bill. She was super and showed me how to become aware of them too - no matter where they were. I just had to be quiet and then think of one or other of them. As I concentrated I suddenly became aware of them - their thoughts, that is. However there were times when I couldn't find them and those times, Julie said, were when they had closed their mind to anyone through emotion - grieving usually, or generally feeling down and low and causing a wall of fog around them so dense that I could not penetrate it. So I used to keep on trying - just like when you phone someone and they are engaged.

Then I would get through and if there was something I wanted to get over to them, I had to use all kinds of tricks really, to get them to know what I was trying to convey. Sometimes, if they had been miserable, I would draw their attention to something in their vicinity that was funny in some way - what a difference in our 'connection' when they laughed or smiled or were happy! When they weren't, it was just like a bad line and I could not really get anything through.

So, in this way, I was able to keep in touch with my dear ones, who were still in the earth life. The years passed and I guided Jemmy through her exams and I was able, in time, to help dear Bill to meet a really nice lady, whom he eventually married, and who became a very good friend to Jemmy, and even produced a new baby - a boy, to take Robert's place.

I decided after much thought, to help Julie, with children who came into this world - who died in some way, sudden or not. I kept my eye on Robert of course, but he soon developed ideas of his own and friends; and I found that somehow, I was often able to be in two and more places at once!

The greatest thing that has happened to me, however, since I died, must be my meeting with Dr. Rossi.

This person was a children's specialist when he was on the earth. He was a very good surgeon and he still has the need to help people in the same way. After many years of relearning the art of healing, he has set up a little group of dedicated souls here and a couple of the same mind on the earth, and together they help people on the earth and off it. I found that my strong abilities to focus and concentrate my thoughts, were one of the most essential attributes to 'Spirit Healing' from this world, and so I have joined this group and together we help where we can.

38

RON

I could hear Brian singing 'There'll be bluebirds over the white cliffs of Dover' and I rubbed harder at the side of the tank. It was taking ages this time. I had usually got more than three quarters of the way down by now. Nobody else in the works wanted this job of cleaning out the tanks, and it was only because I got double time for it that I had volunteered. I was thinking of my holidays whilst I rubbed. In a way I was laughing because this one job alone would pay for our holidays, more or less. It was easy and I had no-one looking over my shoulder.

'Just get them clean, Ron, that's all we want. Take your time, the new shipment's not due in for three weeks yet.'

Funny stuff acid, I thought to myself each time I did the tanks. You'd think they'd be self-cleaning, but our bosses always wanted the tanks rubbing down with this chemical. It was all right for me because they provided me with all I needed - four pairs of heavy-weight rubber gloves, special non-slip boots and a new extra thick waterproofed overall each time.

After the first rubbing on, the chemical turned anything clinging to the side into a deposit which then dropped on to the floor of the tank. So I always started at the top of the tank, after installing the gangplank which went all around the sides. This gangplank was suspended on ropes - it was not too heavy, and it could be raised and lowered very easily. To get it lowered I used a whistle. It was an old police whistle I had from being a lad. My Grandad had been the local bobby and he had given it to me when he retired. I had it in my pocket, fastened to my overall pocket by a button. That way I would not drop it and have to clamber all the way down to retrieve it. When I blew the whistle, Brian would come along with Pete and they would lower the gangplank carefully, with me hanging on to the ropes.

When I got to the bottom of the tank, I usually found two sackfuls of debris from the cleaning. I had all I needed there on the gangplank - my sacks, brush and shovel as well as my flask and sandwiches for my dinner. I rarely stopped for longer than it took to eat my dinner.

Then it all went quiet up top and I knew Brian and Pete had gone for their dinner and a game of darts in the pub across the way. I ate my sandwiches and drank my tea and got on again - rubbing away.

I was making good time when I felt a speck of dirt go into my eye and I suddenly felt a burning, searing pain down one side of my face, and, forgetting I was perched up on the gangplank with only ropes at the edges, I moved backwards with my gloved hands covering my burning eye.

That was all I could remember - nothing more.

I woke up in a hospital with a very hazy feeling in my head and a strange hollowness around me, which I could not fathom. I went back to sleep.

For days I kept waking up and then going back to sleep and during my sleep I kept dreaming I was lying in the bottom of the tank, covered with the mass of debris in the bottom. In my dream I was lying there for ever - no-one came to find me. This went on until one day, I woke up and I found I was surrounded by green. The ceiling of the hospital, the very air below the ceiling, all was a soft shimmering green. It was very relaxing and I found that my head had cleared and I no longer felt the haziness. Not only that but it seemed that I had lost my memory. I didn't know who I was or what I was and there seemed to be no doctors or nurses to help me. My consciousness ebbed away again and I slept more.

I suppose I must have slept for a very long time, on and off. In between I saw no-one and spoke to no-one. Then one day, a voice woke me. It was asking me if I was feeling better. I looked up and there was a small woman with her hair in a bun on top of her head. She wasn't old though - but neither was she young. She wasn't a nurse because she didn't wear a uniform. I sat up and realised that I felt very well and I told her so. She suggested I got up from the bed and took a walk with her.

When I did this I found we were not in a hospital, but in some kind of a park, and I wondered if I had been sleeping outdoors all of the time.

'No,' the lady said, in answer to my thoughts. 'You have been in a kind of hospital for the past two years of your earth time.'

I thought this was a very odd thing to say and said so, upon which she said I had died in an accident at work, but would not accept or respond to any kind of help.

It was a rum going on, really. She was calm and assured but how could I believe this? I never used to tell many people at work, but I was quite religious and my wife also. We used to evangelise around the district on a regular basis, talking to people about God whenever we could.

My religion - my beliefs, told me that when you died you would be met by Jesus or one of his disciples. This lady - for all she seemed kind and gentle - was certainly not what I expected to meet me. She was, and she felt a stranger to me. The only obvious answer to it was that I was not dead - I certainly would have remembered dying because we used to talk about it in our meetings from time to time. We used to be quite joyful thinking of the reunion with Our Lord. It certainly couldn't have been what I had experienced - being in a hospital.

Also she said I had spent two years sleeping! That I just couldn't believe, but you would not have thought this lady could tell lies. She just didn't seem the type.

'Come with me, take my hand' the lady said suddenly.

Without thinking I took her outstretched hand.

'Close your eyes,' she said.

I closed my eyes and had the strangest sensation of movement - as if the ground were spinning under my feet. Then it stopped.

'Open your eyes,' she said.

It was a familiar sight that met my eyes - the room of a house. It was my house, and my wife was sitting at the table reading the Bible. She looked very well and happy and kept looking at the clock to see the time. It was five o'clock it seemed. I looked around the house and noted quite a lot of changes. There seemed to be none of my things about - not even in my wardrobe or drawers. There were suits and shirts, jackets and trousers but they were all of a much better quality than I used to wear. Then I noticed on the dressing table, a photograph of a wedding. It was at our own church and there was my wife

41

looking very happy and alongside her John - my best friend from church.

I couldn't believe it - my wife and John! I knew John was a widower and was in quite a good office job - management really. How was it possible that he had married my wife? Then the door went and someone - John, called 'I'm home, Darling!'

My wife almost ran to the door and threw her arms around him. Well! She never did that for me - not since the early days of our marriage, that is.

'Have you seen enough?' It was the lady asking me. I had almost forgotten her. I hung about a little longer, looking in all of the rooms for just something of mine, but there was nothing. I had been wiped out as if I had never been.

'Close your eyes,' the lady said as she took my hand. This time I opened my eyes to find myself standing in a cemetery. I was drawn to a grave - not at all new, but the grass growing over the mound had recently been cut. I bent down to read the headstone. What a shock! I felt decidedly ill. That was my name right enough and my wife's name - 'In Loving Memory' she had had inscribed on the stone - and yet there she was married again!

'It is two years' the gentle voice at my elbow said.

'I think I am going to have to believe you,' I said reluctantly. 'But there are so many questions - so many contradictions!'

'I know,' she said, 'and I will try to show you in time - that is if you are willing to accept me as your friend and guide?'

I looked at this small lady again, and this time I realised that she was familiar to me in some way. I just couldn't put my finger on it but there was something about her that I remembered.....

ELLIE

Ellie was excited. The aeroplane was full and her own group of forty chattering schoolgirls took up just a corner of the huge cabin. She had never flown before and she had never been abroad - indeed she had never been on holiday before without her parents. The school trip was the first her school had ever tried and everyone had been saving up for a year. It would be nice to see other countries in Europe. They would be able to relate better in Geography, when they had seen and identified with the actual places rather than just books and atlases.

Spain would be so warm, too. She had got some new summer clothes as hers were too small now and quite old as they didn't get much worn. She looked down at her new shoes. Quite grown up really for a ten year old. Just imagine, no uniform for three whole weeks. Sunshine for three whole weeks and they would be walking around soaking it all up before going back to cold weather until their own summer came.

Ellie looked out of the window at the clouds. What a lovely strange feeling it was, sitting up here over the tops of the clouds - in the sky. It was extraordinarily blue up here - apart from the fluffy white clouds below. Such a blueness was quite amazing and in some way hypnotic. She found herself staring at the blue often when she looked out of her window.

She was lucky to have a window seat. They had drawn numbers as there were only so many seats by windows. Of course Grineff could see out of the window too - with no difficulty, but it was nicer to be able to look down the side of the aeroplane and get a different view.

The stewardess brought round hot drinks, or cold drinks and little sandwiches of rolls of bread with some kind of kernel in it. Very strange but interesting. She had two of these small sandwiches and enjoyed them. There were also three different kinds of meat in little slices on the tray which Ellie was balancing on her knee. The food was different and nice - so long as she liked it of course!

There was a buzz of conversation on the aeroplane, but Ellie and Grin were not talking at that moment because Grin was reading a comic and Ellie was quite enjoying her gazing at the blue.

There was a sudden lurch and the aeroplane seemed to drop down a long way - the clouds were rushing past - layer upon layer with bits of blue in between. Ellie's stomach felt funny at the lurch and still was and her head started spinning dizzily - so much so that she closed her eyes in a hope to get rid of the feeling. Then the whooshing stopped and she opened her eyes. Below her she could see mountains - peaks and valleys. The aeroplane was not very high above them and it was possible to see roads like strips of sticking plaster crisscrossing the sides of the hills and the valley bottoms.

Then the Captain's voice came over the Tannoy, asking them to fasten their seat belts as he was going to have to make an emergency landing. The stewardesses came round to everyone making sure they had their belt on and saying they were going to make an unscheduled landing at an airfield in the Pyrenees.

That was the last thing Ellie remembered - the stewardess checking her belt, just before that awful dizziness came back and she closed her eyes. Then it all stopped and everything was very quiet around her. There was no buzz of chattering, no laughing, no engine noise. Just stillness. Her head was still feeling muzzy so she kept her eyes closed and soon she fell asleep.

When she woke up, they must have arrived, for she was sitting in a chair on a golden beach feeling extremely warm and pleasant. Just a little in front of her, the sea was gently lapping against the lovely yellow sand. The colours were beautiful. There were trees around, which Ellie had never seen before. Trees bearing oranges and lemons - but what an enormous size these fruits were! She decided to try one and got up from her chair and walked along the crunchy sand to the cluster of trees. She was easily able to reach up and detach a large, lovely firm orange and she went back to her seat to enjoy it.

Then she wondered where everyone else was. There were people around her but none of the girls or teachers. A bit strange, she thought as she peeled her orange. The sections were large and looked juicy so she popped one into her mouth - what delight! So much nicer than the oranges she had at home and she really loved oranges. She looked around for a bin to put her peel in and found one almost next to her chair. How strange, she hadn't noticed that before!

Just then a girl of about the same age as Ellie came

along, smiled at her and asked if Ellie minded if she joined her. Said her name was Fluke. Strange name, Ellie thought and Fluke smiled again and said she thought she would have an orange too. Once sitting alongside Ellie, peeling her orange, Fluke asked Ellie about herself.

Ellie started to tell her new friend how she had come on the school holiday to Spain. She got to the part when the aeroplane had started to come down to land in the mountains and found she could not remember anything else.

Fluke asked where the other girls were and Ellie was not able to answer. She broke off in confusion.

Fluke told her not to worry and said no doubt they had gone off somewhere and Ellie had decided not to go with them. Would Ellie like to come with Fluke who lived near the beach, and meet her family? So Ellie went off happily chattering with her new friend and found a very lovely house, standing in its own gardens, but not enclosed from everything. Fluke had two brothers and a sister, and several aunts also lived with them - or at least were staying with them for a while.

Fluke showed Ellie her toys and the games room, where all manner of interesting things were going on. They seemed to have lots of pets, all of which had their own little exercise rooms in very large cages with open doors so that the little animals could come and go. It was delightful and Ellie loved this room. She stayed a long time playing with the animals and watching them and praising them when they seemed to do a complicated climb or swing.

Then she turned her attention to the games she could play with the other young members of the family. Again she spent a long time enjoying herself - forgetting everything in the excitement and wonder of such interesting games and toys. According to Fluke, they had all had a hand in inventing the games, toys and machines. It seemed a strange family who got so involved with their children as to encourage them to actually design their own fun. Ellie was all for it, and when someone suggested a pony trek, she was very keen, as she loved horses and had been looking forward to this part of the holiday.

It must have been hours later when Ellie and the others

came back from rubbing down the ponies and seeing they had plenty of water and food after their hard work carrying the friends around the hills. It had been a lovely exciting ride and Ellie looked forward to doing it again. It was still light and bright with sunshine everywhere and Ellie wondered at how lucky these Spanish people were in having such long summer days.

Fluke happily showed Ellie to a room where all Ellie's things were hung and set out. As she washed, ready for tea, she realised that there had been no language difficulties at all - and yet she was not top of her class for Spanish or any of the other languages. She had always been good at sport and gymnastics and found the other lessons at school a bit boring. She never really put in a lot of effort. This always upset her father, who wanted her to be quite academic and go to University and perhaps become a teacher herself. Her mother, on the other hand wanted Ellie to be good at home crafts - cooking and baking and needlework and homemaking. Then she wanted her to find herself a nice boyfriend and get married quite early and have a lot of children. Mother was quite silly really, Ellie thought - so fluffy really and she hadn't much sense, her father said.

Ellie was an only child and the only arguments she ever heard her parents have, were over her. Her parents were each in their own way, very strong personalities - even her mother had a way of getting everyone to do what she wanted. The result was that Ellie often felt very torn between the two of them.

It was a miracle that she had been allowed to come on this holiday. As it happened, her mother had to go into the hospital for an operation, and it had been her idea, so that Ellie's father did not have to hire someone to look after Ellie - or send for relatives of his. Ellie's mother was determined this last would not happen. She did not want them in her house, let alone looking after her baby, as she often called Ellie! Her mother had been an only child too, and her parents had died in a motoring accident a few years ago. This was one of the reasons that Ellie was so coddled and her mother was so possessive of her.

She had never got over the loss of her parents. She was

46

even protective of her husband too and Ellie's father seemed to accept it. Ellie supposed it was because her mother was so beautiful, that her father gave in to her when he did. She seemed to twist him round her little finger.

Ellie dragged herself back from wondering if her mother was all right in the hospital, gave her hair another brush and went downstairs.

Everyone was gathered in a lovely room with a window so large it took up most of the wall, and looked out on to the beach and the sea. There did not seem to be any traffic here, and Ellie wondered if it was forbidden in this lovely seaside village. It was hilly, so perhaps everyone thought it better to walk around and they certainly seemed to walk very slowly, as if they had all day. She had heard this of the Spanish - 'Manyana' - tomorrow will do.

She liked the idea and determined to enjoy every minute of the holiday and not rush about. The children seemed to have plenty of physical activity, so she knew she would be happy here. Then she wondered again about Grin and the others - had everyone been farmed out to different families in different villages? If so perhaps they would all meet up sometime, and in the meantime she was very pleased with her lot.

They all had a very happy meal - so much different from the quiet ones at home. It was not rushed and people were encouraged to talk - to bring up whatever subject they wanted. Ellie really felt one of them, there was no awkwardness at all. It was just as if she had always lived here!

It was much later after tea that Fluke's mother asked Ellie to come out into her garden with her. Ellie got up happily and took Fluke's mother's hand because she felt such love coming from this lady and she felt comfortable with her.

They walked along to a beautiful little flower garden with seats around a pretty pool with little frogs sitting around in the warmth, on the flat lily leaves and coloured rocks. It was a lovely place.

'Ellie, I want to tell you something very important and that is why we have come to what I call my 'magic garden'.

Ellie smiled and sat by her, half-turning so that she

47

could watch Fluke's mother's face.

'Ellie, what do you think happens to people when they die?'

Ellie thought 'What a strange question' and didn't know quite what to say. She began to think about her mother and wondered if there had been bad news.

'It is not about your mother I want to speak, Ellie. It is going to be difficult for you to understand what I will be saying, but try just to listen, then ask what you will. The aeroplane in which you were travelling, crashed into a mountain side, Ellie. Everyone was killed.'

Ellie looked at Fluke's mother and wondered if she was really saying those words.

'Yes, that is just what I said, Ellie. There is no such thing as death because you are a spirit, part of God, and eternal. Only the physical body can die - you, the spirit cannot.'

She then looked into Ellie's eyes. 'Fluke and the others are not really my children in the earth sense. They, like you died from the earth and their earth families - a few years ago. I became their mother here because I love children very much and I try hard to take the place of the mothers they leave.'

Ellie could not speak. She sat there quite numb. She closed her eyes and when she opened them again, she was alone on the seat - alone that is except for a little green frog which had jumped up and even now was sitting there intently staring at her. It seemed to be saying 'Hello Ellie'.

Ellie felt a great lump in her throat and the tears came and flowed down her face and still she could see the little frog face looking at her.

Ellie automatically put out her fingers towards the frog and it climbed up on to them. It didn't feel wet and cold, rather it felt nice and warm and Ellie felt a wave of love all over her as if the little creature knew she was unhappy and somehow was trying to comfort her.

Ellie and the frog sat there a long time, neither of them moving. Thoughts were flowing through Ellie's mind and every now and then she cried and sobbed. As she cried she kept feeling the warmth like a light shining all over her. No-one interrupted them and when Ellie could cry no more and she decided she would have to face the others again, the little frog suddenly jumped straight into the pool and Ellie could see it swimming off to join the other little frogs.

Ellie had a lot of questions to ask and she went in search of her friend, Fluke.

GILES

It was a glorious day. I put my foot down on the accelerator and the car shot off, overtaking the slug in front of me. I felt very good for I had just done a good business deal and I would take my wife out tonight to celebrate. Where shall we go this time? Somewhere different and certainly somewhere expensive - it was a good deal and could lead to a lot more with a bit of luck. Due of course to me! I really have to admit I am a great salesman - better than those two I employ to sell for me. I shall really have to look at those two buggers - I can't carry people and if their figures are not as good as my last month - they'll have to go, both of them. There must be better men out there and I am not a charitable institution.

Yes, it was a very good deal and I feel great. Of course I shall have to cut a few corners for the price, but that's no problem to me. We deserve a really good holiday this year - might even consider buying a villa somewhere in the Canaries. 'That's right - move over - I'm in the overtaking lane aren't I!'

Yes, I've really done well for myself - and Ann of course. Still she deserves it, the way she looks and the way other fellows look! I must admit I like people to see what I've got and what I've done for myself. I liked their faces in the village when we drove through with this car for the first time! They all looked - really turned heads we did!

I always have got on though. People have always envied me for one thing or another. Always got the best in clothes and the latest in cars. Big detached house in its own grounds with a lodge so that people have to stop first there before being allowed up the drive. That's how it should be. Can't have hawkers and such-like knocking on your door all hours of the

49

day.

I work hard for my brass and I want people to know it and respect it of course. Not bad for the start I had - not that I like to think about that. Made the most of my schooling though - passed my scholarship and worked like a navvie at school. Knew just where I was going - to the top. All my own efforts because I knew no-one with any money or position.

Of course, like any other businessman, I had to stand on a few heads to get there. That is the challenge of life. No place for weaknesses of any kind.

So here I am. A success.

I think I will put a little music on to keep up with my mood. There, just a tiny spot to touch and the car is filled with soft muted music. Classical of course - I would never allow myself to listen to the modern rubbish.

Yes, life is great - thanks to myself!

Good God what's that flaming fool think he's doing - 'Move out of my way!' There's a bend ahead - I'll get him on the inside! Oh God, he's moving over now!...........

I can't believe this. I am in absolute agony here and my car is on fire. I am trapped by the legs. I can't hang on....I'm passing out.

'Can't help you staying around here, you know.'

'Who's that?....where am I?....what's going on?'

'You've had an accident - or at least you've caused one and now you've died.'

'What do you mean I've caused one? I can't believe that! Oh I'm in agony!'

'No you're not - you've died I said.'

'Died! Don't talk rot - I'm in agony I tell you!'

'Stand up and you'll soon see who's right.'

'Look, who are you? Where am I?'

'Just get up and walk over here and I'll tell you.'

Suddenly my vision cleared from the mists I felt I was in. I could see the wreck of two cars in a field. Both cars were unrecognisable, having been totally destroyed by fire. At the roadside an ambulance was just about to depart.

'Hold on!' I shouted to the driver and started to run

towards it. I was too late, for the driver didn't see me and the ambulance went off up the road. I turned to the police who were also about to move off. 'What about me! What's happening?' I asked one of them.

He just continued to his car as if I hadn't spoken. I started to get very angry because I wasn't used to being ignored by anyone. I ran towards the police car as the two officers got in.

'They wouldn't have known a thing about that, I reckon!' one of them was saying. The door slammed almost in my face and they drove away leaving me standing there by the roadside.

What the hell is going on?

'I've told you, you caused an accident.'

It was the same voice I'd heard before. I turned round. There was a chap in dungarees - like a mechanic or something, standing there, looking at me.

'Who are you?' I asked him, 'And what the hell's going on here?'

'How many times have I to tell you? You caused an accident and both of you got killed.'

'It was the other fellow who caused it - he wouldn't let me overtake him and then, when I pulled into the inside lane to pass him, he pulled back into it - how can that have been me?'

'Well, that's for you to sort out yourself. As far as I'm concerned, I've come to take you away.'

'Take me away! You're not an ambulance man - how can you take me away, and where can you take me? I should have gone in that ambulance!'

'Well your body did and I've got to take you where you belong.'

'What do you mean 'where I belong?' I think I must be suffering some kind of damage to my head because I can't make out a word of what you're saying!'

Then I must have passed out I think, and when I came round, there I was in a kind of hospital bed. It was a very quiet ward I was in - no doubt private, I thought. At least they realise I can pay for the best treatment, rather than dump me in the casualty ward with every Tom, Jack and Harry Malingerer. Bye, they wouldn't malinger so long if they were paying for every minute and every cup of tea and phone call!

After a while a nurse came along and asked how I felt. I told her that oddly enough I felt very well - I just had a problem with my thinking and memory. She told me not to worry and disappeared saying that someone would be coming for me soon and just to lie and relax as much as possible.

Well I thought it was good advice because somehow I just couldn't clear my thoughts. Suddenly I felt a very warm light coming from the ceiling, shining down on to me. It felt great - like being under a warm heat lamp, when you've pulled a muscle. The relief was the same, flooding all over my body and making me feel really good.

Then it went out and the fellow in the dungarees came to my bed and asked if I was ready to go.

'Where are we going?' I asked him. 'I'm quite comfortable here in the hospital and I might have to have more treatment. I haven't signed myself out or anything.'

'No, I've signed you out in a manner of speaking.'

I didn't like this - in fact I must admit I didn't like him too much either. I decided to tackle him, for I was never one to just go along with things.

'Just who are you and why have you decided for me whether I should leave the hospital?' I asked.

'I'm the only friend you've got at this time' he said.

Friend? I thought, with friends like you, I don't want any enemies!

'Well you've plenty of them!' he said as if he'd tuned into my thoughts. 'Come on, you're all right now, no need to stay in bed any more. The sooner you get things sorted out the better - and there's plenty to sort out, seeing as you've been a bit of a "doer" all your life!'

'How do you know anything about my life?' I asked him as I got out of the bed and looked around for some clothes.

'You have your clothes on,' he said. I looked down and saw he was right. This irritated me because he seemed to have the upper hand over me and of course I didn't like that at all.

However, he started walking down the ward and I followed.

We walked out of the hospital and through lovely grounds. I wondered which hospital it was as I certainly had not been there before.

'No, you haven't been here before - you haven't been to any of the places I shall be taking you, before.' Again I felt the irritation.

'No use you getting all het up because there is nothing you can think that I won't know, as long as I am with you,' he added.

'How is that?' I asked. I didn't want to get too friendly with him because I didn't know enough about him. I never got too friendly until I had had a person checked out. I used a small one-man detective agency for this. I always considered that knowledge was power, and so I always tried to get as much information as possible about those I dealt with. It made me feel good as well. Somehow this fellow had used my own methods on me. I would have to be careful with him, I decided.

'I certainly don't used spies of any kind!' he laughed and I felt more uncomfortable than ever.

We were approaching a riverside, a kind of tourist area. There were seats and small tables scattered around a patch of very green grass. There were trees, and with the blueness of the sky and the gentle dark green of the river, it certainly was a very attractive place - reminded me of some of the villages alongside the Thames. We sat down facing the river and the fellow I was with turned to me. I noticed then he looked quite young and his eyes were very compelling. As he looked at me, I must say I experienced a peculiar feeling which I cannot ever remember having felt before. It was as if I knew the man, but I knew that I didn't.

'I have to get you to realise that you have died.' he said. Just that. He was not smiling, so it was not a joke. I sat there unable to speak because my main belief in life was that you only live once and so you had better get what you wanted when you wanted it. It was every man for himself. I really believed that - it made sense to me. I had no room for religion, that was for the weak. I believed in myself - there was no God or any other such things, no Heaven, no Hell. When you died you died. That was that. Snuffed out like a candle. Gone. For good.

'Work it out. You caused an accident in which two cars were completely wrecked and burnt out. You saw the ambulance take away two bodies - the charred remains of yourself and the other man. No-one could have survived that and no-one did. Think about it. It would be impossible.'

I always prided myself on my clear thinking. Just after the accident, I had felt my mind clouded and I couldn't think straight. Now, however, I felt a crystal clarity in my thoughts - much sharper than I ever remembered before. He was right - as much as I hated to admit it. No-one could have walked away from that grisly pile-up. No-one could have survived it. So......

'I am ready to listen,' I said to him.

If I had expected him to talk and talk I was disappointed because he didn't. He just said 'You are not the body. You used the body to find yourself - to discover who and what you were. Now you will go on doing just that and I am off. I've done my bit. I'll no doubt see you again.'

With that he went and I was left to contemplate the river on my own.

CAROLINE

I awoke to a very loud crackling noise and opening my eyes, I saw the whole room lit up with the red glare of flames. I couldn't believe it for a minute and then, in a panic thought of the children. I pushed the covers away from me and bending low to avoid tongues of flame coming at me from the curtains, I edged round the bed, fear pounding my heart so that I could hear it myself. It was already very hot in the bedroom - the wardrobe and dressing table were smouldering and ready to flare up into flames. I got to the door which as yet hadn't been touched, and on to the landing. That was all I knew because, outside my bedroom was an inferno of flames. I passed out. I knew absolutely nothing of what lay beyond that wall of fire.

My next feeling was that I was in total blackness. There was nothing around me and all I could think of was where were my children - where were Tommy and Carol? I started to panic at the thought of their being as lost as I was. I couldn't remember the fire - it wasn't even a dream in my mind. All I knew was that somehow I was separated from my children and I wanted to find them again. I began groping my way along in this blackness - being careful where I put my feet and spreading my arms out all around me. Like this I seemed to move quite a long way, but as yet there was no light for me to get an idea just where I was.

Then I seemed to hear someone calling me Caroline....Caroline..... I stopped to listen and all of a sudden I could see a figure just in front but still a long way from me. There was some kind of light around the figure which got brighter as the figure got closer.

With joy I realised this was my father! Dad, who had been killed in the war, just a few years ago. I ran towards him with my arms outstretched. Dad and I had always been good friends as well as father and daughter. My mother had at times been a bit jealous of our closeness for she said it seemed to cut her out. I didn't feel much for my mother, and even when Dad had been killed, I felt sorrier for myself than for her. Then I left home early to get married. What a terrible mistake on my part! Harry just didn't have what it takes to be a father and husband. It didn't take him long, after Carol's birth, to clear off with somebody. Then I got no money or word from him at all. That was four years ago and now.....

Dad's arms went round me and he was saying how sorry he was for being so late.

I asked what he meant and where were we, but he just took hold of my hand and said 'Close your eyes, Caroline.'

I did as he said and I felt and heard a whooshing sound, and, suddenly I felt light on my eyes, so I opened them and there we were, in a lovely garden with a few swings in a little ring where Tommy and Carol were swinging away as if they'd been there forever.

'Hi Mam!' Tommy called out, and Carol nearly fell off

55

her swing as she let go one hand to wave to me.

I breathed a sigh of relief for some reason - I didn't know why at the time, and turned to Dad and said, 'Are you a ghost, Dad? Have I become a spiritualist or something, being able to see you?'

He laughed. 'No, lass. Come and sit down on this bench here, where we can see the children and I'll tell you.'

We sat down on a nice seat - it must have been new because it was really clean - not like park benches usually were! I wondered which park it was and how we had got there. I certainly didn't remember a park in our town like this. It was so clean - that's what impressed me most about it, and the colours were so bright. The grass and the flowers were really brilliant in their colours.

Dad started, 'It will be hard to take this, Caroline, but you were all killed in the fire at your flat. It was the biggest fire they had known and everyone in the four flats died - no-one got out.'

I stared at my Dad because it didn't seem to make sense and yet, how was I sitting here talking to my father who had been killed in the war? I just couldn't remember the fire. The last thing I knew was that I had gone to bed a bit earlier than usual because I had a headache. I'd taken a sleeping pill in case I couldn't sleep and that was the last I knew. I thought I'd had a dream where I was walking in a very dark place with no lights at all and I wanted to find the kids. Then Dad came along.

'You would never remember the fire, love. Your mind would blot it out from you so that you would not be distressed. There would be no point in your remembering and here, you only know and find what you can make use of. A bit later on you might begin to remember bits, but not while you're a bit stronger in yourself.'

I tried to focus my mind on Dad and forget myself, because the kids were happily playing there in front of us, so I had no worries about them, so I asked him what had happened to him.

'Oh, Jerry got me. I was one of a group of four and we had to take a jeep across the Belgian border. We hit a mine and then, as it didn't go off fully, a party of Jerries came and shot us all.'

'Did it hurt Dad? It sounds awful!'

'Oh no,' he said. 'just like you, I didn't know what the heck was going on. In my case I was still there but watching it all. I followed the Jerries back to their camp and saw all sorts of things I shouldn't have, I suppose. They were just like us really, you know. I seemed to understand their talking, and, in listening to them, I realised they had the same worries and problems as us. They really wanted to be back home with their families. I went back to my own regiment and learned a few things there as well. I knew I was dead though and I found it very interesting, realising that I could move around as much as I wanted without my body, which I had seen below me after the shooting. Then I thought about you at home and Hey Presto I was there! I was around you all the time. I heard all of the rows and all of the laughs and I tried to get you to hear me, but by then you had met that Harry bloke and I had no chance!'

I was very fascinated at all of this and he went on and told me one or two things which I didn't think anyone knew about! Still I must say I felt very happy sitting there with Dad, watching the fun Tommy and Carol were having. Then I thought about the future and said to Dad, 'What's going to happen to us, now Dad?'

'D'you mean where are you going to live and everything?'

'Yes. Are we going to live with you? And how will we manage for money and such?'

'Well, love, first of all, you don't need money here. You will have what you need as regards house and everything. You won't be living with me though as I've got a lot of work on at the moment. I will be coming to see you quite a bit at first, but, as you get sorted out, you'll make your own friends and then maybe you'll get something to do as well.'

I began to wonder why it was that we all three had died so young, and so I turned to Dad, but he started talking before I had a chance to get the words out.

'Don't worry about things you can't help,' he said,

'here, in this world, because you will find it is a real world, you know. Worries are taken away from you. All you have to do is think for yourself and make a life. Get interested in things that you didn't bother with before - try different things and talk to different people. Don't get involved with people unless you've looked at them properly.

One thing is that people can't tell lies here - everybody can see what a person's like if they look. Like your thoughts - be careful what you think because everyone can read your thoughts you know! That's how I knew everything you had on your mind.

I'm going to go now and let you find your own way about. It's not good to do too much for people, you know, especially when you care about those people. The more you do for yourself - you'll see, the better you'll feel about it and the more confidence you will have. These are little rules which, if they were followed on the earth, would make life there so much better for folks.'

Dad got up then, and although I was wishing he would stay a bit longer, he walked off, calling 'Cheerio' to the children.

I sat on a little thinking over what he had said. It seemed that I had another chance to make something of my life. I know that when Harry had gone, although I was really glad to see the back of him, I didn't rouse myself much. I took the flat on even though I knew it wasn't a very nice area. I wanted people around me no matter what those people were like. That's probably what Dad had meant about my not looking at people properly.

He'd always said I should have made a bit more effort at school, because I had a good brain and I should have made use of it. I didn't though - I always wanted to be liked by the wrong people, so I hung around a crowd that got up to all sorts except learning!

As I sat and thought back, I realised that I had never really set myself any goals in my life. I was being given another chance. This time I could really have a go!

PAULINE

I used to work in a factory, when I was alive like you are. It was a good job - well paid and a lot of fun. It was fun because of the girls you worked with. There were a few fuddy-duddies of course - wouldn't be a world without them and you always made a bit of fun of them, in a kind rather than horrible way really. If they were ever in trouble we would all stick up for the fuddy-duddies just as much as for one of your mates.

Well, I am here to tell you what happened to me the day I died. It was an accident really - at least that is what people call such happenings, but really I know it wasn't.

I was cycling to work at about half past five one morning. It was Friday and I was looking forward to the weekend as usual. I had just recently met a new bloke at the Mecca Ballroom, and I was thinking about him as I pedalled away down our street.

When I got to the crossroads, I looked quickly to my right and saw nothing and pedalled straight across. I didn't look left at all and I had my head down as I had racing handle-bars. The next thing I knew was I heard a big bang and felt my bike go up in the air and me with it. I was only a little 'un - just five feet tall and thin with it. So I felt myself go up and that was that. I never came down. I never knew another thing.

I heard later that I'd got concussed and was taken to hospital. It was a lorry I'd had my tussle with - he'd come to the junction a bit fast and when he saw me doddling along, it was too late to stop. What a shock for him! He was not hurt at all of course, but my bike was crumpled up like a concertina and I was out like a light. There wasn't much blood on the outside but I had suffered damage to the brain. I was in a coma.

There was a special ward for brain damaged people at the hospital. My parents and the lorry driver - for he came to visit me as regularly as my parents did, though not at the same times - were told by the specialist there, that he did not give me much of a chance. He couldn't operate on me, and I had tubes everywhere and an oxygen tent to help me breathe. The damage had been very severe as my head had been caught by the back wheels. My eyes were open it seemed but I did not register recognition of anyone. Everything really had to be done for me - there was no self-motivation at all.

Now the very strange thing was, that at the hospital, I had come round to myself. I was in the emergency operating theatre, being tested for all kinds of responses by the surgeon and I suddenly became aware that I was looking down at myself from somewhere up near the ceiling. I felt quite well but looking at my body I could see that it wasn't functioning at all - nothing really was happening there, apart from the gentle breathing helped by the oxygen tent.

Suddenly I felt very sad, because I knew that my body was never going to be any good again. I was going to be a crippled person - even a cabbage it seemed. No more dancing, no more factory - nothing. I felt a sudden depression coming over me and I blacked out.

I will never forget my Mum and Dad's faces as they looked at me for the first time. It had taken the police a while to find out who I was, as I had no identification on me. I never used to take my handbag to work - just a pack of sandwiches to eat in the canteen, and a spare hanky.

It was night-time when they brought Mum and Dad in a police car. What a shock for them. I had come round just before they came in and felt awful because I couldn't move any part of me. Then seeing their faces, I began to cry. The thing was, my body wasn't crying - it wasn't doing anything. I couldn't even feel my own tears....but I could feel my mother's and my father's! Imagine my father crying! I had never seen him cry in all my eighteen years!

It was terrible to see them and to be able to do nothing about it. I just had to lie there - not even blinking. They didn't know what to say to me. They thought a lot and somehow it was as if they were talking to me - sometimes both at once! I wanted to tell them not to talk at the same time - but they weren't and I couldn't. I also wanted to tell them that they were wrong in thinking I must be in agony, because I wasn't. Nothing hurt - nothing at all. It was just not being able to move that got to me.

They sat there a long time that first night. The nurses brought them a cup of tea and later a cup of coffee. Dad kept looking at the heart machine recording my heartbeat - watching the red line being traced round the drum on the graph paper. He was dreading it stopping, I knew.

Mum was remembering all the things I used to say and do when I was three. She kept going back in time to our holidays and the photos and the concerts we used to do at school. Typical of Mum really. She lived in the past.

Later on Geoff, my brother came along and Peg my sister. They were both so shocked it upset me all over again and I got depressed and again I blacked out. I missed the rest of their visit.

The next day, very early in the morning, along came the lorry driver. He looked worse than my parents! I had realised that it was thoughts I was hearing - not words and his thoughts were very strange. He seemed to believe that this accident was something he deserved - even though it had happened to me, not him. He felt so guilty that I realised he would suffer for the rest of his life. In that respect I suppose it HAD happened to him. His thoughts were not very pleasant at the start. He was a bullying kind of man I found - he didn't care what he said to people. The nurses were not fond of him and didn't bring him tea or coffee. Half of him didn't want to come to the hospital but his other half did.

As he sat by my bed looking at my still face and staring eyes, he started to think of a daughter he once had. She, it seems had been knocked down by a hit and run car. They never found the driver of it, and his daughter had been killed outright. He had vowed to find that driver somehow and beat him to a pulp. I was sure he would, too, because his thoughts were black enough whenever he thought of him. These thoughts of revenge outweighed his guilt. He only stayed half an hour - just sitting there, not speaking out loud, but thinking such a jumble of thoughts.

I stayed like that for a week - seven days, and my family and the driver visited me every day. My family used to talk to me - never really expecting me to reply. The driver never ever spoke.

Then all of a sudden, on the morning of the eighth day, I knew my body was going to die. I wondered if it would hurt. I wondered if I would just go unconscious. My thoughts were just starting to get morbid when I noticed that the little red line had come to a stop and so had the rise and fall of the oxygen balloon. I waited to go into unconsciousness....but nothing happened. I was still alive. I was still thinking and seeing. I realised I was up near the ceiling again, looking down on my body. A nurse had come in and looked at everything and rushed out again.

The doctor came in and checked pulse and heart. They removed the machines and the nurse put the sheet over the face of what was my body. Then I panicked a little and felt myself. To my relief I still had a body - I was solid and by now was standing by the bed, feet firmly on the floor. It was a big puzzle to me. I didn't know just what was happening at all.

Then I was aware of a dimming of the lights around me - it was almost dark, and a brilliant light appeared in a corner of the room. I wasn't scared for some reason, but I found myself staring as the light became a person. Such a person!

I had always believed in God, even though I didn't go to church much - just at Christmas and Easter and of course weddings and baptisms. I hadn't been to any funerals as none of our family had died. This person I was seeing now was just as I imagined Jesus to look. His face was so lovely - not feminine but so really nice and loving, if I can describe it that way. I felt very drawn to him and that he had come especially to see me. He came nearer and I was standing in his light, which felt very warm to me, very comforting and strengthening somehow.

Then he told me that I had died.

He didn't seem to use words as such, but somehow he passed the information to me. I just knew. At the same time his eyes held mine and I can never describe the look in his eyes! I felt that look.

I know all of this sounds very odd, and as if I was a religious nut, but I wasn't. I hadn't ever thought of dying - I mean who does? It was something that happened around you, I suppose, but you never think of it happening to yourself - of your life being cut off short.

In that look which seemed to last for ages, I felt that everything was all right. That this was as things should have been and that I had somehow come back home!

Part of me though wanted to be back with my life and my other body - even though I had accepted from this person standing there still, near me, that it was all over. Part of me felt it wasn't fair - I was only young and hadn't really had a life. As this argument raged inside myself, the light dimmed again and the 'Jesus' person disappeared.

The hospital room became visible and I could see all that was happening. My body was put on to a stretcher and taken off down a long corridor. The nurse was ringing someone on the telephone and I was surprised to find it was our family doctor. I suddenly found myself there in his surgery as he was taking the call and he wrote in his diary my name and address. Then the room went round in a spin and I found myself at home.

The house was not the same. Mum and Dad were both lost in their own worlds. My brother and sister just didn't know how to be or how to treat everyone else. It was a strange jumble of emotions, guilt, arguments caused by the strain. There was no peace, no happiness - this one event, big as it was, had completely broken up a family's relationships with each other. I didn't like it at all and tried hard to comfort my mother who was taking everything so deeply. I used to stand by her and put my arms around her - but I know she didn't feel me. No-one was aware that I was there.

Then I began to think of the driver and the room darkened and I felt dizzy. When it was stable again, I was in a strange house. There were only the driver and his wife. He had given up driving and was at the moment unemployed. He smoked and drank a lot, he was in a bit of a state and although his wife, being too timid, didn't argue with him, there was no happiness there. She, it seemed had a little part-time job at the corner shop and from what I could gather, was very glad to get out of the house and away from him. The atmosphere was so depressing there, that I too wanted to get away.

Into my mind came a picture of my friend Betty at work. I thought about her, her lovely sense of fun, the giggles we used to have at the factory, and then again I closed my eyes and I found myself at the factory sitting right next to Betty in my old place. It was a bit quiet in there though. No-one was cracking jokes and giggling. Over all there was an atmosphere - like when you walk into a room and the talking just stops. Some of the girls, I noticed were feeling quite sad about me. They had not all been my particular friends, but they were sad none the less. Betty was in a very gloomy state and didn't speak to anyone. Then the forewoman Vi came round asking if they wanted to get a wreath or cut flowers. She asked Betty and she suggested a wreath from the factory. The forewoman asked Betty if she wanted to organise it, but Betty was too depressed.

It was all so miserable and I saw no point in lingering there, and as I sat, I thought about the vision I'd had. Could I see this figure again, I wondered?

I could hardly believe it when the room darkened and the brilliant light appeared once more. This time he held out his hand for me to take. He seemed to be asking if I had had enough of the world I had left - and I think that I had, but I seemed to think that if I took his hand, I wouldn't be able to see my parents or my friends again. His answer just seeped into my mind. You may come back whenever you wish. Your life is as always yours to do with as you want.

'Will you explain things to me properly?' I asked him, and, as he told me he would, I took his hand.

I felt a great surge of strength and obeyed his request that I close my eyes for a moment. When I opened them, I was sitting on a grassy bank, with lovely bright buttercups and daisies around me. Sitting next to me was not my 'Jesus' person, but another man - this one dressed normally - and very attractive looking with a really nice smile. The interesting thing I noticed was that he had a faint look of the fellow I had recently met at the Mecca.

He said,'You wanted explanations, I gather?'

'Well I can't understand just why I had to die as I did - why couldn't I have got better?'

'You had too much damage to your brain to get well again. You wouldn't have wanted to be just a vegetable for the rest of your days would you?'

'No, but why did it all have to happen, when I am so young?' I persisted.

'Well you were the one who was careless and didn't look where you were going. If you had looked and seen the lorry coming, and stopped until it had gone, then you wouldn't be here, would you?' He seemed to be studying my face as he said this.

I had to admit to myself, that he was right - I couldn't blame anyone but myself. 'What happens now?' I asked.

'Whatever you want to happen.' he answered.

'Do you mean I have free choice?' I inquired, quite surprised.

'We ALWAYS have free choice, but do be careful what you choose, this time. Think just what you really wish to do with your life. It really is in your own hands.'

'Who was that vision I saw? The one in the brilliant light?'

'He was someone who was observing you in your life from time to time. He came to you because he felt you needed some help.'

'Will I ever see him again?' I asked.

'I'm sure you will. When you get little ideas coming into your mind - things you have not been thinking about yourself, I think you will find that is him, putting ideas your way.'

'Why should he watch me and want to help me?' I asked.

'You will have to ask him that yourself, when you next see him. Now you really ought to decide what you are going to do with your life.'

'I want to get a few things absolutely clear in my head first. I am dead - really dead, aren't I?'

'Your physical body is dead - which means that your physical life experience is over, but there is no such thing as

65

really DEAD. No-one can really die. Everyone is spirit energy - part of God - and so because God IS, then you will live for ever. Now because you have finished your life on earth, you must get on with your life here. You can choose just what you wish to do. If you choose something you need learning for, then you can have learning. It is all up to you.'

'Is life here much better than on the earth then? I wasn't able to do ANYTHING I wanted to do there!'

'You were able to do a lot more than you realised. It is a case on earth of people liking to fit in moulds and believing all they are told. If you believe you can do a thing, then you will have a go and do it eventually. Such is not encouraged on the earth. You are educated to think you are not good enough for many things.'

It all seemed a lot for me to take in and my friend realised my thoughts and got up saying, 'Come on, I'll show you around.'

I got up and walked along beside him. I felt there was a lot to learn - but if I could NEVER die - then I had plenty of time to learn it in. I felt quite mixed up - I wanted to be back with the life I knew and yet...there was something very interesting here...something I wanted to find out about. After a bit I will go back and see everybody and in the meantime I will try to enjoy what there is here.

I felt quite odd really but my friend seemed to know my state of mind and gave me some kind of strength and help to keep my mind and thoughts more on a level.

'Don't worry' he said, 'most people are like you when they first arrive here. You will soon find something to interest you, and then you will not be pulled hither and thither.'

As he spoke I realised what it was that caused me such feelings. I felt my parents, family and friends - and no doubt the driver too, all thinking about me and wishing I was back there with them. Surely they wouldn't want me to be back with a body that couldn't do a thing for itself? Surely they wouldn't want that for me?

'No' my friend said, 'what they want is for themselves - they miss you and would feel much better if you were there. As it is they all have to learn to get along without you, and all you were in their lives. They have to learn to readjust - just as you have here. Such a happening is a lesson for all concerned - not just for yourself. Like the ripples on a pond, the death of some-one on the earth, has far-reaching effects. It will tell many people about themselves, and that is what life is about - people learning about themselves - the way they think and act and feel at every experience that comes their way.'

ALFRED

It was very noisy on the bus. It had been a good match and so everyone was in high spirits, our team had won, and here we were on our way home. There were the usual cans and bottles of beer passed around. We had stopped off at a roadside pub and we had a good sing-song and of course a good drink. The match had been replayed a score of times and a score of ways. In all we were as happy as could be and we had nothing in our minds but how grand life was.

Then everything changed in the time it took to blink. Our coach was going over a high river bridge, and, without any warning whatsoever, it careered wildly across the road and straight over the low parapet wall of the bridge.

Of course we hardly realised what had happened until that flying down through nothing and then the impact as the coach hit the water. By that time we had all been thrown about - heads smashing against seat backs, and for some this brought unconsciousness, they never knew anything more. For others there were moments of panic - but at a distance, as if it was happening but through a curtain of haze. Of course the alcohol had brought about a kind of stupor, so no-one really was aware of the harsh reality of how they died. The shock of the cold water as it seeped in and the final desperate struggle to slide open the door, were all people knew before their consciousness mercifully closed down and they became unaware of what was happening to their physical bodies.

In my own case, I came to sitting on the top of a hill, it seemed. I know I had a good view of everything about me. There was a lovely deep valley with the usual slow river flowing across it, and trees along the edges of the river. I wondered for a minute or so, just what I was doing up here. There was no-one around me. I had no memory of what had recently happened to me - or even that I had drowned. I tried to get my thoughts together, but I couldn't really get anywhere with them. It was like losing your memory, I suppose. Somehow I had to think clearly, and I realised that sitting up here on my own, was a good place to fathom it all out. I didn't know how I had got there so I had to begin from there.

Who was I for a start? Then as I held this thought in my mind, the scene in front of me changed and, instead of the valley, I saw a dock with a ship alongside being unloaded. At once I felt all right because there I was working on the dock in a very familiar scene. That's it - I was a dock worker. I watched myself and the others finish our work and go off together to the dock gates and make our various ways home. I saw myself cycling along the streets until I got home, where I saw my wife and family, and I realised just who I was and where I had come from.

However, the scene before me changed back to the valley and a thought came into my head - what kind of person am I? I said this question out loud because I found it a bit peculiar. Ordinary, I thought in answer to it. I'm just an ordinary bloke, in an ordinary job, with an ordinary family.

Then I nearly fell off my hill because the scene before me changed again. This time, somehow, it went back to a time when I was a lad. We were at the swimming baths, one Saturday morning. I enjoyed swimming and had got on well with diving and over-arm. I had just completed a length of the bath and was standing on the edge, when, at the other end I saw two burly lads throw a small third boy into the deep end, then jump in on top of him. They then swam off, not even bothering to see if the little one was all right. He wasn't! He hadn't come up and I ran down the bath and dived in and swam to the spot. I had to dive under and keep my eyes open, but I had practised

68

this quite a lot and was able to see fairly well.

The lad was lying on the bottom. I got a hold of him and propelled him up, and as quick as I could, to the side of the bath. I then jumped out and applied what I remembered of artificial respiration. I'd had no training in life saving, but I had seen others practising around the pool.

Fortunately someone had gone for the attendant and the boy was wrapped in a blanket and taken care of. He was all right. The attendant came back to thank me for my rescuing and said he had found out the culprits and reported them to the police. This scene faded away then.

Strange I had forgotten all about that episode in my life. I pondered over it but could not think much about it. I had only done what anyone else would have done in my place.

Once again the scene below me changed. This time I was watching myself getting quite drunk on the occasion of my eighteenth birthday. I smiled to myself as I recalled the situation I was observing. I really did put back some stuff that night. A pity really because there was a really smashing girl someone had brought along, and, at the beginning of the evening, I had decided I would chat her up. Then somehow things took their own course and I finished up blotto, no girl and very, very sick! What a waste it had all been. I never saw the girl again - what a pity......I was thinking about her when all of a sudden I saw her in a bank.

She was working as a bank teller and as I watched, she got promoted and promoted until she became the very first woman bank manager, the company had appointed. She became very successful and eventually got on the board of the bank. Amazing really when she had come from an ordinary working class background, just like me! She had a wonderful lifestyle - nice car, nice house - no husband though....well, I thought I must have missed out there. Perhaps if I'd married her, I, too, might have done something better than working on the docks....oh well, no good thinking.

The scene was fading out - interesting what might have been. Then I held my breath because another scene was opening up. There I was, with the foreman, walking to the office.

Then I saw myself and the boss, in his office. He was offering me a foreman's job. I saw myself pleased and accepting, but watching I didn't feel excited, because I remembered only too well what happened. Yes, there I was in the pub with the lads. There were two of the biggest skyvers on the dock buying me drinks - and lacing them. Yes, well, no need to go into all of the details of that short time as foreman.

However the scenes were relayed before my eyes - all of the embarrassing situations as I allowed those men to manipulate me to their own ends. My own weakness for the drink and the comradeship. The walk to the bosses office again and the words from the boss. I was lucky I was not losing my job - he was saying.

Then followed scene after scene. My whole life with its wasted opportunities because of my need for alcohol and friendship. There were also scenes that showed me in a good light but at those times I didn't really realise that this was as much my true self as that other.

There were many scenes projected there, that showed a totally different path I could have gone. Then, finally came the football trip. I saw my wife suggesting a holiday in Switzerland for a change. She would get it all organised, then we could go together and get our passport photos taken. I didn't fancy going abroad for a holiday and said so. Anyway, the football trip had been organised, and I didn't want to miss that with the lads - it was only once a year after all. In the end my wife went to Switzerland with her sister - and I stayed home.....and went on the football trip.

I was quite a long time sitting there. Time though didn't seem to matter - no one was counting. I don't ever remember doing so much thinking. I came to the conclusion that every-thing in life concerns making decisions - choices in fact. Everything that then follows is a result of those choices. There was no-one else to blame. I made all of the choices.

I had died when that coach careered across the road and over into the river. I know that I died many years ago, where your time is concerned - but it takes a long time to look at yourself properly. I never looked at myself when I was a dock-er. I just went from event to event - good, bad, indifferent. My drab life was my own choice, I can see that now. There were opportunities to change it, all along the way. I just happened to ignore them.

In my life now, I am doing my very best to try to persuade people like myself, to take those opportunities as they come along for them on the earth. If you are anything like I was, I might just whisper in your ear from time to time - you never know!

THE SKIER

When I was asked to join a small group skiing in Switzerland, I was not sure I wanted to go. However I went.

It was a good flight and the weather in Switzerland was bright with a strong sun, and quite warm for the middle of winter.

Our hotel was good - very comfortable in fact, with lots of little luxuries which make it seem like home for us Americans. Seated on the balcony with a nice cocktail in my hand, along with a number of good friends and jovial company, I began to feel pleased I had come along - it was going to be fun after all.

Our guide then joined us - although we were all very experienced skiers, this hotel always insisted on a local guide. The snow, according to the proprietor, did not always finish up in quite the same place - especially if there was a wind. So then it was not possible for anyone to really know these slopes - they were high and they could be tricky.

OK, we all accepted Hans with as much grace as we could muster, feeling quite like schoolchildren whilst the hotel boss was talking to us. Then Hans stayed with us to get to know each and every member of the party - he was a thorough guide - and a thorough gentleman, I might add.

Our very first day proved disastrous and indeed the last for several of the party, including myself.

There had been several fresh falls of snow during our convivial evening, and the next morning, when we assembled on the slopes, there was a fresh wind moving it all around. Most of us were quite chirpy about this, because it promised us a good run down with a bit of a challenge. Sure, it would be tricky for a first day, but no-one would take risks - we all had declared we would just take it easy and break ourselves in gently.

Our guide, Hans, announced that he would lead us off, and although we all six looked at each other with a smile under our scarves, we had promised to play it cool this first trip down. I was third after Hans and as the descent began and Hans swerved round the hill sides, the usual thrill began to creep over me.

It happened so quickly that I could not really remember how it all went. Hans swung just out of my sight, I followed Bob, who was just in front of me in his bright green ski suit. In front of him, I caught a flash of red as Pam disappeared from sight. Then it seemed as though I was falling, falling, down through soft snow. Down, down, down, it seemed to be a never ending fall. As my speed got faster, my head seemed to spin and then I felt dizzy and remembered nothing more.

It was a strange feeling when I came round. I was actually back in the hotel, in my bed. I looked out of the window at the falling snow and thought I had been dreaming that we had gone up already. I got out of bed, showered and dressed in my ski suit making sure to wear my extra body warmer. I went down to breakfast, looking forward to the day's run.

What a surprise I had, for it was not morning, and there were only three of our party in the lounge. The atmosphere was awful and I heard one of the three - a girl I didn't know, called Jan, saying that she really wanted to get back home more than anything. She suddenly burst into tears, and her pal George came along and put his arm around her, trying to comfort her.

I went up to them and said 'What's happened here?'

No-one answered me - in fact no-one seemed aware that I was there. I repeated my question, going close up to them. I put out my hand to the arm of the other girl, Judy. She too seemed very close to tears. To my amazement, I was not able to make contact with her arm. There seemed to be nothing substantial for me to touch.

Then in came the hotel owner, saying he had made the arrangements with the Embassy and all was in hand. With him came a guy who seemed to be a newspaper reporter, who wanted to speak to one of the three, but they were not having any, and told the guy in no uncertain terms, to go.

Then I was aware that I could read the thoughts of George, as he sat with the two girls, waiting for the Ambassador to arrive. It was quite late in the evening, and again it was snowing hard outside. As I looked at the window, it seemed as though I was also out there, in the snow, and there was an automobile coming up the hill. It was making slow progress due to the swirling snow - visibility must have been bad but I was well able to discern even those in the automobile. Strange how I was doing several things at once with absolute clarity.

George was in a state of shock. He could not believe what had happened that day. As he had been next in line to go into the abyss, something had warned him, and he had swerved to the right and stopped. Even then he was in a daze, not quite accepting what had happened to the three of us and the instructor. The other two were a little slow in getting down and so George had made his way up the hillside a little, in order to stop them going down. He just persuaded them to turn back.

He did not even allow himself to go down to see what he could see, because he knew that no-one would have been visible to the eye - just a hole in an area of snow - a hole that went way down.

Back at the hotel, it seemed, his grim news had set into motion a flurry of activity and phone calls. Soon a rescue party had got together and they had gone to investigate and see what they might find. However, to their great surprise, the route taken had been the one skiers never took - a sheer drop to the valley bottom. Thousands of metres down to rocks - nothing more.

So I learned what had been my fate and that of my

companions. Everyone was totally amazed that such an experienced instructor and skier - a local young man who knew these slopes like the back of his hand - should have led the way off the safe side of the mountain, straight down into the gorge.

I tried to get myself to the place of the accident, but somehow I could not, I seemed to be blocked from even a visual view.

It was at this time, as the consul was talking details with George and the others, that I was aware of the presence of a man. It was an old man who somehow had a very familiar look about him. He reminded me very much of my maternal grandfather, who had been one of my greatest friends during my childhood. I had never really understood how he had gone from my life.

I had never been a very religious person. Death really meant nothing to me. My life had been one of struggle to maintain a standard of life I thought I needed to have, alongside all of my friends. Oddly enough, I had hardly any contact with those I termed 'religious' - they just had no place in my life. I had been a fashion model and then a newspaper employee. I was not a reporter, but as a kind of middle person, I set up contacts and meetings for the reporters on my newspaper. It had been an interesting and even exciting job at times, as I travelled around the world to perform introductions to top people, so that we could really get a foot in the door.

I was always very active. I hardly knew what being still meant. People were always in my life - they were my life blood and I was never given to sitting around thinking about myself - or indeed about anything. I suppose I was 'instant' everything

As I looked at this silent figure, who was looking at me with a smile on his handsome, kind old face, I found I was reading his thoughts. He was greeting me without speaking! He had smiled at my own recollections of him. It WAS my grandfather and he invited me to walk out into the gardens and sit down to talk.

I was a little surprised as I preceded him through a doorway - I found myself in a most beautiful garden, in brilliant, warm sunlight. My grandfather ushered me to a seat, in front of which a lovely fountain, bordered by the most colour-ful flowers and plants, seemed to tinkle its water gently down to the basin. We sat, and for the next age, it seemed, my grand-father talked and I asked questions.

It was hard to believe I was 'dead'. I used that word to myself, to make me realise it was a fact. I knew my grandfather had been dead for more than twenty years, yet here he was, animatedly talking and smiling. As I studied his face - tanned as it had always been, due to his love of outdoors, it seemed to me, less old. At first I had assumed he was old, as that was how I had known and thought of him. Now he was looking a lot younger - but still my grandfather - fascinating!

As he talked about his present life and what would be mine, I seemed to forget all about Switzerland and what had happened there. It was very evident to me that I was, somehow, no longer in that country. People were around us, but in the dis-tance. We were absolutely private as we talked.

Then I started to take stock of myself. Whenever I used to sit for a longish period, I had started to get a kind of cramp in my thighs, which made it essential that I get up and move about. My friends I had confided in, all said it was because I hadn't known how to sit down for two minutes together, and now I couldn't. Well, as I sat with Grandfather that ache was not present. I felt down to my thigh to reassure myself I had a thigh, I suppose, and my grandfather smiled and said that I had no need to look for that worry anymore, for I had a new body, which had no problems, as had my old physical one.

Then he stood up and said it was time to meet some other people. Of course I was delighted, loving meeting people as I did, and we moved away from that charming fountain, with its lovely, relaxing, musical water.

PART TWO

Part Two features the experiences of people who have died because some part of their physical body has given up or worn out. In Catherine's case, she had just gone into the hospital for tests to see what was causing the tiredness she had almost always felt.

There are two cases in this section, though, that are quite different in the way that I received them. The experiences of Jack's death, as he sat in his chair by the fire, were told to me face to face through Alan's trance mediumship. It took place years before I began the automatic writing.

Jack had a problem, a very common one, it seems, both on the earth and off it. He could not see himself as he was.

Like most of us, he always thought it was someone else causing the hiccups in his life. Apparently, until Jack was able to see himself exactly as he was, he could not move on to more pleasant surroundings.

Matthew's story, also via Alan in trance, is in two parts and is opened by Uriel, one of a group of people who all died in the nineteen sixties. These people, from all walks of life and all nationalities, decided to band together to try to help the newly dead and the earthbound. They all use pseudonyms - in humour they chose the names of the Archangels, and they are all devoted to their work.

Matthew was an earthbound soul, living an extremely lonely life - which must account for his willingness to hold a conversation, often not very pleasant, for over an hour with a ghost!

I was the 'ghost' according to Matthew, and it was not an easy situation because he was a crotchety old fellow, and I didn't like him too much! It was not easy talking to him, and I had to ask for a bit of help and inspiration from the other side to keep my end up!

However, as you will see in the second sitting with Matthew (of which I had no prior warning), there were interesting results.

CHRISTINA

It was a warm night. The bedroom window was open and I could see the curtains flapping in a gentle breeze. The room around me looked patchy. I could see the outlines of some of the furniture, but there were some areas that were just blackness. Then, in the blackness I could see a spark of light.

The spark seemed to flicker a little and then it grew in brightness. I stared at this spark and wondered what it was. I could still see the area round it, and so I knew I was not imagining what I saw. At the same time I heard a tune in my head. It was an old song 'Beautiful Dreamer' and it came from my childhood.

I had piano lessons when I was very small and this was one of the early tunes I learned to play. I smiled to myself as I thought of the number of times I played it. Every visitor who came to the house had to stand there in the front room and listen to me. It must have driven my parents mad - over and over again! If I stumbled over a note or made a mistake, then I would start right from the beginning again - determined to make a flawless performance. My mother always said I ought to go on to be a concert pianist, because this need for perfection was no doubt what such a performer needed!

The spark meanwhile seemed to be getting bigger. It was an uncanny experience, and I didn't want to miss anything, so I kept focussing on it. Then in my head I heard a tuneless whistling. Good God! That was our old milkman Charlie! Every day he used to come along smiling and whistling like that. He and the whistling were a big part of my world when I was young. I remembered the day I had cause to be very grateful indeed to Charlie. I had gone out on my bike, even though I had been told to stay in our street and tenfoot, I had decided to go round by the street at the bottom of ours and into the next street along the road. I wouldn't have to go out on to the main road, because there was a convenient passage through at the top of the next street, into ours again. This was the route I would take. So, off I pedalled. I would have been four at the time.

All was well until I rounded the bottom street and turned left into the next street. I almost fell off my bike because standing right in front of me and blocking my way, was an enormous dog. It took up the whole of the pavement it seemed to me. I sat there transfixed, one foot on the ground, and the dog and I stared at one another. He was winning though, because I had started to cry with fear.

Just then Charlie's tuneless whistling sounded and he came out of a garden gate, and, seeing the problem shooed the dog away, right out of the street altogether. What a relief! I was able to pedal on at speed till I got to the passage which connected the two streets.

All of the time I was thinking these things, I was watching the now glowing area of light. Then a thought came into my head which I tried hard to dismiss. It stayed however and gradually developed into an incident which I did not really want to think about. My part in that was not at all admirable. I had cheated someone out of their rightful place. During my life this event would come into my mind on odd occasions, but I always managed to find an excuse for my behaviour, and so get rid of the thing. Eventually I forgot about it all together. Why has it come up again I wondered?

A picture came into my mind with most of the details of the incident, but this time I felt as though I was the person who had been usurped. It was strange how I seemed as though I was feeling their feelings. Somehow I was on the receiving end of the whole thing. It was not pleasant and I wanted very much for the thoughts and the pictures in my mind, to go away. They didn't for a while though and so I hardened myself as I knew I did whenever I was in a situation I didn't like. I pushed the thing to the back of my mind and actually closed my eyes.

That always seemed to work for me and it did on this occasion. However this time there seemed to be a lingering thought that the thing would return and return until it was dealt with.

This kaleidoscope of past events went on and on. Sometimes I quite enjoyed the recall, but there were a lot of times when I felt decidedly uncomfortable with it and closed my eyes and ears so that I didn't experience anything but blackness. At such times I seemed to sense a warning in my head 'Be careful!'

It was a very strange experience and always the shining patch of brightness held my attention as the pictures faded and a new one came along. It was a bit like being at a cinema, I thought. Not all of the films you went to see were as good or as pleasant as you thought before you got in. The difference here was that it was all a bit too personal for my liking, yet, how could I get out of it.

As I started to think of getting out of bed, I realised that my body felt a bit heavy. My arms and legs seemed to be quite dead and I couldn't seem to be able to move them at all! I was just beginning to worry about that when the light became brighter and glowed a rich golden colour. I stopped thinking about moving and relaxed again, gazing at the brightness. A bit of colour had crept into the light - a faint rose colour, striped with gold - what a lovely effect! As I watched this I began to feel very light and happy.

Then into my mind came a very happy period in my life - the pictures were brilliant and I felt again all of the joy I had experienced at those times.

Then I seemed to think about my late husband a bit. I seemed to get his thoughts during our married life together, on occasions when I had presumed him to be feeling and thinking as I had been. It was interesting really, to realise that George had seen the simplest things so differently from myself.

He had been a busy man, he had begun a small shop which had become a large shop and then expanded into branches all over around us. Of course I had helped where he needed me, but I must admit I had my own interests and could not get as involved as he did. Here, though, I was seeing it from George's point of view. He wanted us to work together and then when things had been built up, to sell out and move off to a quieter life somewhere, a gentler pace so that we could go into old age as a pair of people who shared everything and enjoyed each other's company.

Then I realised that George was a bit impractical, really.

I asserted my own feelings and ideas once more, and was quite able to see things in a more realistic way.

George never seemed to worry what people thought. He didn't look after things the same, and he didn't care how he looked or how the house looked and the garden. It never bothered him if a friend called and the place was a bit upset. He didn't seem to know that people judged you by what they saw and by what you had. It was no use having a business and going around like a tramp!

We always argued on this score of course. I liked nice things and I liked things nice. George wasn't bothered. He used to say things were just to use and it didn't matter what anyone else thought about it. There we always disagreed but I wouldn't argue after a certain point with him. He just had no style.

My mother used to say I would never find anyone good enough for me. She was right - I never did. None of the men I knew really appreciated the finer things of life. I liked to wear the very best of clothes, even if they were expensive.

People judge you by the clothes you wear, and the friends you have. That was another bone of contention between us. George had some very weird friends. Not the kind of people you could introduce to others. Poor, they were. I suppose. There is nothing wrong in being poor, I know because when I was a child, we were poor ourselves. But life is to get on and improve your lot. Things come your way and you have to make the best of them. I am proud to say I have always worked hard and made efforts to improve everything I have done and had.

This bungalow for instance. If we had gone George's way, we would never have bought it. Stockbroker Belt - that was on the sales brochure. I knew that that was just where we should live but George thought it was too expensive and would take too much out of the business. What was the good of having ten shops, I used to argue, if you had to live in the poorer areas of town all your life? I will admit that our other house was not really in a poor area, but it was not Stockbroker Belt.

Then of course I had joined a few clubs, firstly ladies clubs and then I decided it would help business by learning to play bridge and golf. At first George was reluctant, then he agreed and we eventually made friends of a different type - a better class of people, I thought.

Although our life certainly changed, our relationship - our marriage seemed to get worse somehow. We didn't argue more, we just seemed to live separate lives. I found myself a bridge partner, Nancy, a widow, and George became more interested in the golf.

It was a great shock, when George collapsed and died on the golf course. After all he was only sixty six at the time. He was wanting to sell up still and yet I couldn't see why he didn't just appoint someone to run it all for him and keep the business. He was very stubborn though, and would never see it my way. So he went on, and then this great shock for me.

It took me ages to get over it. There was so much to sort out, I remembered. He really was a messy worker and I had a job getting it all untangled. Really the debts he had allowed the staff to run up here and there! I would never have got a half of it had I been soft like him. As it was, I let a few people off the hook, because they were in a desperate state. I could not imagine how people could live as they did - using someone else's money to pay for their pleasures! I was brought up to believe that if you couldn't afford it, then you didn't have it.

I arranged a very nice funeral for George, and got him a lovely seat in his memory at the crematorium. I made sure that the brass plate would always be polished, also to have the seat regularly varnished - strange that I had to have a legal document made up to provide for this - as well as pay separately of course. You'd think the crematorium would be glad to make sure such things were cleaned as part of the job!

Life was certainly different without George. I really missed him and I had to learn to drive even! We had a car out there in the garage and no-one to drive it, and I didn't want to have to rely on taxis all of the time - you never know who these taxi drivers were!

Gradually I changed my life around and I must say that having someone to run everything, and myself attending a board meeting of sorts every month, things went very well. Of course we were taken over after a few years, and then I was very secure with good investments. Pity poor old George missed the pleasures of life and only had the hard work. He would have learned to enjoy the luxuries I am sure if he had been spared. He collected such a motley lot of people around him though. He was a soft touch really for anyone with a sob story. It didn't get him anywhere though did it? Dead at sixty six! Poor old George.

The light now is becoming a different colour, and I think I can see some kind of figure building up in it. Good God! My mother! Well I can hardly believe what I am seeing! I can hear her voice as it used to be when I was young. She is calling me like she used to do. The room now has a very strange light all around it, and is beginning to get a bit misty, but my mother is still standing there, by the bed with her hands stretched out to me. She certainly looks very nice in a lovely long dress of pale colours.

It must be a vision I am having! I am beginning to feel a little odd. It must be the effect of my sleeping pill working at last. I feel very relaxed and sleepy but at the same time the room is beginning to move away - my mother too. I will close my eyes I think, because I am feeling quite strange, as if I was dropping down ....and down...and down...

MR.POLLIT

It was a nice Spring day and Mr. Pollit and his wife had just caught the bus into town. They were on their usual shopping expedition, that they carried out each Saturday. They went to the same shops and bought the same things - there was rarely any variation on this routine. Mr.Pollit could make the journey with his eyes closed, he felt.

The bus turned into the bus station and Mr. and Mrs.Pollit got up and joined the line of people moving down the aisle. Just as he was about to step off, Mr.Pollit felt a stabbing pain in his chest and suddenly he crumpled up and dropped down to the ground. At the same time as this happened Mr.Pollit felt himself step over the crumpled form, which he thought was someone else, and then turned to see what he could do to help the unfortunate man.

There was a bit of a shock for him when he realised that it was in fact himself! Things seemed to happen quite slowly after that realisation. His wife had stepped back into the bus and someone was helping her to sit down by the door. The bus driver had jumped off and gone to the office to telephone an ambulance, and people were standing around in little groups, wondering what they could do to help. There was of course nothing they could do, and when the ambulance arrived, Mr.Pollit's body, which had been declared 'dead' by the ambulance men, was loaded on to a stretcher and put inside the ambulance.

His wife was helped into the ambulance, and Mr.Pollit himself got in too, and sat beside his wife and the ambulance man. His wife was extremely white and the man was anxiously asking if she was all right. Mr.Pollit tried to comfort her as best he could, but somehow he was not able make any kind of physical contact with her. He could not understand at all what had happened. He could not really be dead because here he was, quite solid and feeling reasonably well.

He certainly had gone a bit funny after the pain in his chest, but this had worn off now and he just felt he had to clear his head to know what to do next.

At the hospital, a doctor came rushing over to the stretcher and checked the heart and pulse of the body, and then gently pulled the blanket over the head. He turned to Mrs.Pollit and led her into a small room. Mr.Pollit followed and sat down with his wife on a settee next to a small table which had a pretty bowl of flowers on it.

Soon a nurse came along with a cup of tea for his wife, and the doctor, after checking that Mrs.Pollit was as well as she might be with the shock she had sustained, left the room.

Mr.Pollit sat with his wife and realised that she had been struck quite dumb with shock. Her mind seemed a blank to him. He knew suddenly that she was going to faint and he turned to the nurse to warn her. Although the nurse did not respond to him, he felt that she, too, realised that his wife was not as well as she seemed, so, when Mrs.Pollit slumped back in her seat, the nurse was able to administer to her at once.

It was decided to keep Mrs. Pollit at the hospital for a while, and they took her to a small ward where a nurse put her to bed. Mr.Pollit had been able to keep up with all that was going on, and whilst the nurse was putting his wife to bed, he discreetly went out of the room into the corridor. To his consternation, he was still able to see into the room, but at that moment he heard a doctor coming along to check her over.

Not knowing what to do, Mr.Pollit hung about for a while. The odd thing was that people just were not aware of him. They passed through him, as if he was not there, and they didn't hear him when he tried to talk to them. On the other hand he was very much aware of them and what they were saying to each other. He knew the doctor had given his wife an examination and then a mild sedative to help her sleep for a while. He also knew that his body had been taken to the mortuary and put into a drawer with his name on it. His clothes had been taken off and an inventory done. His name and address had been given to the police, and a policeman had arrived to wait for his wife so that he could take her home. So much activity going on and he was totally helpless to do anything he considered useful.

Later in the day, his wife was back home and sitting in the living room, on the settee, staring blankly in front of her. Messages had been sent to the family and he knew that their three sons and their wives were making plans hurriedly, to get over to their mother's side. He was even able to be aware of their feelings.

With one it was grief at not having been there. With the other two there was a tinge of irritation at the inconvenience of it all. He was surprised, because the one he had expected to be sorrowful, was not and the one that was, he had always thought was uncaring. Because he was interested in these reactions, he found that he was able to be in the homes of his sons and their families, and so he knew first hand just what they were feeling and saying even! This quite threw him and he sat down on a chair at his elder son's very respectable house and passed his hand over his eyes for a moment.

He had never been an emotional man himself, but there was a degree of family loyalty to be expected. It was a bit of a shock to him to realise each of his offspring's feelings. This set him off on a train of thought and before long he found himself like a fly on the wall at the homes of several of his friends - or at least those he thought of as friends.

News certainly travelled fast and Mr.Pollit seemed always to be just ahead of the news of his own death. People were very much different from what he had always imagined - that was for sure. He was beginning to think that dying was a bit of an eye-opener! When he actually thought this, it brought him up sharp. He was sitting in the Walker's Arms. This was his local, where he met his friends and colleagues at the bowling club he belonged to. He had been drawn here when his closest friend Bill had been informed of his death. There was a group of his friends all standing now, quiet and with their heads bowed in respect for him. It would have been quite moving had he not known at the same time, the thoughts of these three men.

Bill was thinking 'God, it could happen to me like that, having had that check-up and the doctor saying I had to take things easy!'

John was thinking 'I can't believe it - here one day and gone the next. I wonder who will make the team up now?'

Eric was thinking 'You never know when it's your time. Poor old Harry!'

None of them had really been touched though. It was like reading a newspaper - it had happened to someone else and no-one really cared so long as it wasn't them and they were not too inconvenienced.

It was then that Mr.Pollit thought about the fact that he had, in truth died. How could he be here like this - seeing but unseen? Was this what the Spiritualists knew about? What was his future now? He felt himself and knew that he was solid - it was a very odd situation, but as he felt all right in himself, it was also very interesting.

85

He decided to return home and watch over his wife. She would need some strength and perhaps, somehow, he would be able to do something. The idea crossed his mind that this might well be what haunting was all about. Maybe there were millions of people hanging about their former homes and families, trying to help them along. Mr.Pollit decided that this was just what he was going to do - not haunt or frighten anyone, because he couldn't do that. He had never been one to push anyone around or to instill fear into any of the people who had worked under him at the factory. He might be able to bring about good things for the people he knew. It might be very interesting being 'dead', he thought - it certainly was not something he could change in any way, but he might well be able to be useful.

So Mr.Pollit died and yet continued to live just where he had always lived, and went from time to time, to the same places he had always gone to. He seemed to get a degree of pleasure in observing life. One day, however, when he allowed some little opening in his routine that had taken over after his death, someone would come along on that side of life, and try to persuade him it was time to move on and away from his old haunts.

CATHERINE

At last the visitors went and Catherine was able to lay back on her pillows. She couldn't go to sleep yet, though, because there was supper to come and then the toilets and the wash before settling down for the night.

The ward was noisier than usual and when her supper came, Catherine wasn't really hungry. She only tasted the meal and then pushed it away. Of course the nurse would have something to say, but she was far too tired to bother.

It was an effort to hobble off to the toilets and to get washed at the row of sinks, but she managed it on her own, and with a clean night dress on and a little talcum powder, she felt nice and fresh. She sank into her bed and pulled the covers over her shoulders. Oh, what bliss to be able to go to sleep at last! It was always a long day in the hospital, because they were awakened at six o'clock with a cup of tea.

Catherine had come in for tests. She had been in for tests before, because there was something wrong with her blood, they said. She wasn't really bothered, because she had always felt so tired, living was really an effort these days.

Her family were always telling her to rally round and get well. They didn't know what she felt like, so how could they tell her what to do? It had come on gradually since her husband had died. She had spent a long time looking after him, with his chronic chest problems and it seemed to her that she had given all she had in doing so.

She had always suffered some health problem herself, but had not really gone down with any one thing. Life had always been a bit of an effort for her, from being quite young in fact. She never really felt that vitality that Arthur had before he became ill. He always used to be dashing around here and there. He always had to be into everything that was going on, but often the mere idea of it tired her - even when they were first going out together. She had hoped he would settle down once they were married - but he hadn't. A real live wire everyone had called him!

It had irked him when he couldn't get his breath and was forced to stay home. He became very irritable but Catherine just took it all and only rarely argued with him. It was never worth it. He had such a quick temper and she couldn't stand the shouting. Arguments exhausted her more than anything.

Her family were always trying to get her to go here and there with them and the grandchildren, but she always managed to have some health situation when these excursions cropped up. Then she could stay at home and potter around in her house and garden. A lot of people were like her, surely - not everybody wanted to go gadding about? One place looked very much like an other, and one person sounded very much like another.

She was only sixty seven, but she certainly felt older this time in the hospital. The tests had exhausted her and she was prescribed a few tablets to help build up her blood and vitality. That last was a bit of a laugh, she thought as she waited to go off to sleep. The doctor had said that they would soon have her jumping out of her bed wanting to get home.

She wanted to go home, all right, but she wouldn't be jumping out of the bed! She didn't expect the tablets to do anything for her - they hadn't in the past, why should they now?

Her breathing became deeper - at last she was drifting off to sleep.

It was a nice, warm day, and Catherine was ambling gently down a very long lane. It was shady with trees down one side and a nice hedge along the other. There was a gentle slope upwards and she took it slowly, enjoying the fresh air, the singing of the birds and even the walking. Funny really, she didn't usually like walking and had refused to join the Ladies Rambling Club when her friend asked her. Maybe she was wrong, and she should join it, because it was really very pleasant going along here - even with a bit of a hill to walk up.

On and on she went, taking in the countryside around her - gently rolling fields, mostly green, no doubt young crops growing there. The trees were in leaf and looked lovely - their greens and coppers mingling together. There was blossom on some, and in the hedges were wild roses and wild flowers in abundance.

On and on she walked and soon came to a small wood with a few paths meandering through it. She left the road and walked on the springy turf of the wood, among the trees. Now and again she would stop and watch some squirrels as they played merrily up and down the trees. They seemed oblivious of her so she was able to get a good view of them. It was lovely this walk - Catherine was really enjoying it.

A small brook gurgled through the wood and Catherine stood at the side and looked into its shallow clear water. There were a few little fish swimming along, reminding her of when she was very young and her brothers caught tiddlers at the park.

Then she was out of the wood and back on the path. The brook had become a full ditch running alongside the road and from time to time she stopped to look into the deeper water.

All of a sudden the road opened out on to the top of a moor, and, to her delight there was a seat at the highest spot with a lovely view from it. She sat down with pleasure and looked down at the sloping fields and the various birds and wildlife. It was very pleasant sitting there in the warm sun. She really relaxed.

Then she thought she heard a voice calling her name. She listened, yes, there it was 'Catherine'. She looked around her but there was no-one in sight, so she realised she must have imagined it. Perhaps she was becoming a bit drowsy with the warmth. She closed her eyes as she sat, because it felt the natural thing to do, and there, in front of her eyes it seemed, she saw her husband's face looking at her. He wasn't smiling, but he wasn't sad, just looking. She opened her eyes wide again and got up deciding to walk on.

She had no idea where she was going and somehow it didn't really matter. She followed the path down the other side of the moor, enjoying the countryside. At one spot there was such a breathtaking view of a valley, that she found a seat and sat down again. Her eyes took in the view and then gently closed again. This time she saw her family - their faces all seemed to be looking at her, all solemn and sad.

'Mum' they were saying. How strange! She opened her eyes and after taking another look at the view, off she went.

So Catherine walked for mile after mile. She never felt tired. Her feet never once bothered her. Now and again she would sit on a convenient seat and the inevitable eye-closing would happen. She would see her husband's face, her various children's and grandchildren's faces, then she would see her friends' faces. Sometimes she saw the faces of strangers - and all of them called her name. It was very strange and she couldn't understand it, so each time she would rise and continue her walk.

Always the countryside was different and interesting. She didn't feel hungry, although she must have been walking for hours and hours. It was as if she was making up for all of the walking she had missed in her life. All of the outings that she wouldn't go on before.

Then she thought of towns by the coast that she could never be bothered to visit, since her children had grown up. Then somehow she found herself at Blackpool, walking along the front. It must have been early in the morning because there were no other people about, but it was warm and pleasant. She was able to look at all of the shops and entertainments as she walked the whole length of the Golden Mile and then further.

Then she thought of Brighton and Scarborough and other places and each town she visited and walked for miles - again not seeing a soul. Whenever she sat down and closed her eyes, back would come the faces saying her name. Her thoughts strayed to other countries she and Arthur had discussed and some they had visited before the family had come along. Again she found herself visiting them, exploring and walking, peering into shops, sitting watching the sea, never feeling the least bit tired.

Then, on a visit to London, she was sitting in the Tate Gallery, in front of some paintings. She was happy and relaxed and she felt a presence by her on the seat. Startled she turned and saw Arthur sitting there. This time he was smiling at her.

'By Cathy, you've been hopping about a bit, haven't you?'

Catherine got up quickly and walked out of the gallery. She thought of home and almost at once found herself in her own chair at home, by the fire. That was a bit of a shock she had experienced, Arthur being there and talking to her. How could it have happened, she wondered.

Something made her look up and there he was again, sitting opposite her in his old place. This time he didn't speak but just smiled at her.

Catherine stared at him, wondering if he was a ghost.

'No, I'm not a ghost, Cathy. You really are seeing me,' he said, still smiling.

He looked very well - even younger than when he had died. Reminded her of their younger days.

'Why not look at yourself?' he said, indicating the mirror over the mantelpiece.

Catherine got up and looked in the big mirror there. The face that looked back at her was hers at the age of thirty or so. That had been her prime, she had always thought, for looks and figure anyway. That was before she started feeling so tired.

Arthur had got up and was standing by her. He took her hand.

'Sit down again, Cathy. I want to tell you something.' He gently manoeuvred her down into the chair. 'Cathy, do you remember being in the hospital for tests again?

'Of course I do,' Catherine said. But really, she had only remembered that when he asked her. Before that she had not even thought of it.

'Well, love....you died there. In your sleep. You just went to sleep and you died.'

'I don't remember dying,' Catherine said puzzled.

'No because you just went to sleep and dreamt.'

'Dreamt?' she asked.

'Yes, don't you remember your dreams?'

'I remember walking for miles through the most beautiful countryside and then travelling all over the place. But how are you here, Arthur? Where are we - I thought I had come home?'

'You have come home. I have been with you all of the time, trying to get your attention, but you were enjoying yourself too much - you ignored me. Even when it was your funeral, I tried to show you the family, to try to make you investigate what you were seeing, but you just went on with your walks.'

'I remember seeing the family - they were looking sad, but it was too lovely where I was - I hadn't realised how nice it was walking. When did it happen?' Catherine asked, looking a bit worried.

'Well, you will be surprised - it was a year ago.'

'A year!'

Everything went dark for Catherine - just as if she had fainted. The shock had sent her into a deep sleep. It would be refreshing to her, but Arthur would have to start all over again, to get her to realise that she had really died in her sleep, that she was not dreaming the whole.

MATTHEW

(This sitting took place on February 1st 1988)

URIEL: Good evening. I will only speak to you for a moment and then depart - I will leave the end result for you to consider, unless you wish me to return to discuss the events?...I shall do that then, to talk things over.

Now this individual - I must admit to a little deceit at this point, he doesn't really know what he is coming to. I haven't told him that he will be speaking to someone who is not on his own level. That is for him to find out, but basically speaking, from his point of view, he will become aware of you. He may well consider you are the apparition!

This is something beyond his previous knowledge. I have, of course, told him that life does continue after death. He doesn't really accept that he is in that position. His life hasn't really changed too much.

You will find yourself in the position of someone who appears to his senses, and then we shall see what transpires. Your role I think, will be to convince him that he is the one that is the apparition of course - and not you! You will find that an unenviable task, because you, in some respects, will not be able to prove it. In some respects you are an apparition to him because you are in a different condition, the same as you are to me - although you don't appear to me with a clarity that you would consider acceptable.

He will be able to see a vague form and not with a hundred per cent crystal clarity, and that will be the difficulty that you must try to overcome.

This is a way of demonstrating to you, the problems we have, so you will perhaps understand a little, the difficulties that many of us do meet, and hence why some of us spend a great deal of time in what is called, I understand, the 'Dark Regions'. There is nothing dark in them in the visual respect - it is merely a lack of mental illumination. It is just how people view it.

I shall depart and hope you find it interesting. He will of course be under the impression that he is merely sitting at home, but we are guiding his mind somewhere else. He realises - he has been asked, that if he will sit and relax for a little while, it will be beneficial to his normal condition, which, although he is not ill, he is the sort of person who tends to be a little tired most of the time. Not surprisingly, of course, it's through boredom more than anything else.

So you will appear to him. He won't be polite of course, in the strictest sense of the word, by bidding you 'Good night', because after a certain time, I shall just withdraw his thoughts and apply them once again to the world he inhabits. You will disappear from his imagination but of course it will give him something to think about when I next speak to him.

In case there are certain points you do not understand, he may well view me as a social worker. I view him, of course, as a social shirker - but that is besides the point....

ANDREA: Is his state of mind as it was when he first died?

URIEL: We have got him to this point. He is amenable to a bit of suggestion that may improve the quality of his life, but you will find that he is......plodding along - and that is the best way to put it I think. He has turned the corner to opening his mind to certain possibilities to help him relax, and, with the administrations of various evangelists who call upon him from time to time, with certain thoroughness, he does tend to consider a few things which perhaps he hasn't done before.

He doesn't accept of course, that life after death exists and that is where we are directing you to. You realise of course, that this is his condition. He is a somewhat basic individual and doesn't really yearn for anything better - this is his difficulty.

ANDREA: Did he die this century?

URIEL: Oh yes. There is no difficulty there. I think he has been dead for approximately thirty years, from your point of view, so that is not too bad. The world he lives in is somewhat imaginary, because the people he knew still exist for him, and that of course is somewhat tiresome. Although he may well be simple in his requirements, he has recreated his world that he was living in - he was on his own, and he still carries on in the same sweet way. If the vicar used to call every Tuesday at a half past two, well sure enough there he is on the dot, saying the same old things, nothing new - and so he just continues.

We guided him on different walks, and it has just confused him a bit. He says 'Didn't recognise this place - must have done a bit of work since I passed this way.'

It hasn't made him think too much though, he just incorporates it into his routine, so we must be careful what we tell him otherwise it becomes a part of his myth.

However you shall see for yourself, I hope. So I shall return in a moment or so. Until that time I shall leave you to it. Just wait a while as I don't quite know how we shall attune his thoughts through the medium. It may well be difficult, but it won't be impossible or I wouldn't be talking to you now. It is merely getting his vocalisations and mannerisms as best we can.

There was a lengthy silence here and then I saw Alan's body take on a very different way of sitting.

ANDREA: Good evening.

(Alan's body jumps startled.)

VOICE: Good Lord!

ANDREA: I said Good evening.

VOICE: What.......what, what, what are you?

ANDREA: What am I? I'm a lady. What are you?

VOICE: Where have you come from?

ANDREA: What do you mean? This is where I live.

VOICE: (Shouting) No! No it isn't at all - I live here!

ANDREA: No you don't!

VOICE: Yes I do! Lived here all my life! Don't tell me that! Where have YOU come from!

ANDREA: Are you a ghost?

VOICE: (whispering) Are you a ghost? (Louder) YOU'RE a ghost! Good grief I've never seen anything like it! No! Of course not!

ANDREA: What do you mean 'You've never seen anything like it? What can you see?

VOICE: Well it's....What can I see?.....Well it's just

94

mistiness...it's a form...it's vague...what do you expect me to see?...a ghost - that's what you are, a ghost....of course you are!

ANDREA: That's a laugh - you're the ghost!

VOICE: Ha! Oh yes? No I'm not...you're....just sitting here, minding my own business.....appear out of nowhere!

ANDREA: Did I? Like the Cheshire Cat?

VOICE: Quite so.

ANDREA: What year is it, where you are?

VOICE: What do you mean - what year is it? Nineteen fifty three!

ANDREA: Fifty three! It's nineteen eighty eight!

VOICE: (laughs) Well you can believe that - believe what you will. I am just sitting here - just relaxing. It's all that fellow's fault - 'Just sit down and relax' he says, 'you'll feel a lot better'........lo and behold!

ANDREA: Well you do feel better don't you?

VOICE: Of course I don't - you frightened me to death!

ANDREA: I'm sorry about that. What's your name?

VOICE: Well you come appearing out of nowhere! You can't expect anybody to feel all right after that!

ANDREA: Well you're not on the telephone else I'd have rung you up.

VOICE: Well you're hardly likely to ring people up! Ghosts don't ring people up - they just appear, move things around and then disappear again. Just like you. Oh yes!

ANDREA: Well, what's your name then?

VOICE: Matthew. Haven't you come to tell me anything?

ANDREA: I've come to tell you that you've died.

MATTHEW: I'm not the apparition! I've got news for you, I'm solid, real! You're the misty apparition! That is certain.

ANDREA: Well, the reality that you have is different from the reality that I have - because you've died and I'm on the earth - alive.

MATTHEW: Then why aren't I misty? You're the misty one!

ANDREA: I'm misty to you, but I'm very solid to me,

95

just as you're very solid to yourself. We're in different worlds.

MATTHEW: Then why aren't I in Heaven if I've died - or Hell? You tell me that? You're so clever!

ANDREA: Heaven and Hell are states of mind.

MATTHEW: Why don't you go away! Why don't you go to Heaven? What are you doing here in my house?

ANDREA: I'm not in your house - I'm in my house.

MATTHEW: (angry) No! It's MY house. I've lived here all my life. It's not yours. It can't possibly be yours.

ANDREA: What did you do for work?

MATTHEW: Why?

ANDREA: I'm just interested.

MATTHEW: Thought ghosts were supposed to come and tell me things - not ask questions!

ANDREA: Well, I've told you something. I told you that this is nineteen eighty eight, February the first.

MATTHEW: Well that is not worth listening to....totally wrong! 'Course it is, partly right, of course it's February the first....

ANDREA: Oh, is it? That's interesting....but nineteen fifty three...

MATTHEW: Quite so. You're getting it right now. You'll get it right eventually. Obviously dying's disturbed you in some way.

ANDREA: Does it disturb people when they die then?

MATTHEW: I imagine so, not quite being the same is it? No!

ANDREA: What is dying then?

MATTHEW: What do you mean 'what is dying'?

ANDREA: What do you think dying is?

MATTHEW: Exactly that - you've died! Strange question!

ANDREA: Well, it's only the body that dies, isn't it? You, your mind, yourself - you can't die.

MATTHEW: Rubbish!

ANDREA: It's not rubbish. Your mind is closed.

MATTHEW: What else is there? The physical body! Here I am physical! You're as bad as that preacher that comes

96

round! Physical this....

ANDREA: I'll ask you a question then. Do you ever suffer with backache? Indigestion?

MATTHEW: Now and again. In the morning. When I get up. Always have suffered from my back. It's from lying still in one place - locks it.

ANDREA: Do you go to the doctor, then?

MATTHEW: Not very often.

ANDREA: When was the last time you went to the doctor?

MATTHEW: Oh about a year ago, I think. Yes, just feeling a bit jippy and I went in and he gave me some medicine - that's all. Nothing wrong in that!

ANDREA: Were there a lot of people in the surgery?

MATTHEW: Oh, three or four. Mrs. Higgins from around the corner. She was there with her little boy. Pimply-faced little thing. Measles I think. Spreading it around! She should have kept him inside! Then there was that stevedore with a broken arm. He was there.

ANDREA: We don't have stevedores now - everything goes by container.

MATTHEW: Containers - what are you talking about?

ANDREA: Well everything's changed at the docks now. You don't have stevedores. They have enormous containers which are lifted off the ships by cranes, on to lorries. You don't need stevedores.

MATTHEW: Don't you? Well, that's your problem - nothing to do with me - is it?

ANDREA: Well it is because you're the one who's thinking there are stevedores about.

MATTHEW: Of course there are! Who's going to do the work?

ANDREA: I've just told you. Everything is packed in containers that are lifted by a crane into the ship's hold. You don't need stevedores - you have crane drivers. You're thirty five years out of date.

MATTHEW: Rubbish! Nothing on radio about all that!

ANDREA: Radio? Have you got television?

97

MATTHEW: No, I don't have television - newfangled thing! Radio's good enough for me. Keeps me in touch.

ANDREA: Well there's nothing on your radio because you're out of date. That's the problem.

MATTHEW: You're a strange sort of ghost. Are you prophesying the future - it might be worth writing down, this.

ANDREA: Well, write it down then. You might become famous, you know. Has the Queen been crowned then?

MATTHEW: Yes, of course. Only the other day.

ANDREA: I'd like to tell you something about the Queen. She's sixty now. Her son, Charles, who is Prince of Wales, is married.

MATTHEW: Rubbish! He's just a boy!

ANDREA: No, He's in his late thirties...

MATTHEW: I don't know why you're making all this up! I don't know why you don't go away if this is all.....it's rubbish! If you're going to say something, say something that can be proved. If you're so right - why don't I know it?

ANDREA: Because you're dead, that's why. You've finished your time on the earth. You're just going on thinking you are just as you were. Your mind is closed and won't accept anything else.

MATTHEW: If that were the case, If I was dead, are you saying Mrs. Higgins is dead as well?

ANDREA: She might well be.

MATTHEW: That's why I can talk to her as I'm walking down the street? Oh yes! I imagine that the young boy who delivers the papers, he's dead as well is he, and therefore when he places the paper through the letter-box as he goes past - he's dead is he? Oh! Very interesting!

ANDREA: What I am thinking is that you have carried over your habit patterns from your life. They are so strong in your mind, being a creature of habit, that you keep it all going.

MATTHEW: Rubbish! Absolute rubbish! Of course it is! I mean if that is the case well, habits change - good habits, bad habits alter. You're telling me that in thirty five years I haven't changed one jot! Rubbish! Utter rubbish!

ANDREA: Do you think you have?

MATTHEW: What?

ANDREA: Changed.

MATTHEW: Compared to what? I haven't passed thirty five years - that's what I said! Thirty five years one expects a change - I haven't changed! Thirty five years haven't passed! Of course they haven't!

ANDREA: They have. This is nineteen eighty eight.

MATTHEW: You're saying the Queen's sixty odd - rubbish! Rubbish! Absolute rubbish! Well, I don't know why you're saying these things - they are so blatantly untrue. So blatantly untrue - absolute drivel!

ANDREA: I don't think you examine situations very well. You turn a blind eye to things.

MATTHEW: Not a matter of a blind eye - I don't know what you're talking about - examining situations! Plain as the nose on your face! Turn the radio on, they don't say the Queen is sixty three...don't say that her son is married himself - he's only a little boy!

ANDREA: He's got children of his own - eldest son is about five.

MATTHEW: Absolute rubbish! I don't know why you're saying all of these things - obviously you're not a good spirit! I'll have to have a word with the vicar - get the place exorcised! This is the sort of thing he warned me about! Evil things! Obviously you're evil - you're trying to send me round the twist! Drivel! Poppycock!

ANDREA: Princess Anne is married with children as well.

MATTHEW: I don't know who you think you're trying to convince with all this - you probably believe it yourself! Undoubtedly if you were on the earth, you were probably in some asylum somewhere! You just come out of nowhere expecting me to believe all of this rubbish!

ANDREA: You can't really believe you just die and that's the end of it? What would be the point in life? Life has purpose.

MATTHEW: Well take you! You're dead obviously you're a ghost. What is so special about it if you carry on?

ANDREA: I've come into life for a purpose as everyone has.

MATTHEW: Come into life! You aren't in life so that's academic isn't it?

ANDREA: I am in life. I couldn't be talking to you if I wasn't in life.

MATTHEW: Well your not in life or you'd have a solid form, wouldn't you? I'd see it wouldn't I?

ANDREA: Well everything is energy, and you're just a little faster in frequency then I am.

MATTHEW: You do live in a world of your own don't you? I suppose that's your idea of death - living in a world of your own! I shall get the vicar round to have a word with you - get you exorcised. Send you on if there's somewhere to go on to - Heaven or wherever -

ANDREA: How can you believe in exorcising people if you don't believe in life after death?

MATTHEW: Well you go to Heaven or you go to Hell and that's where you stay. If you're good or you're bad. If you're indifferent I don't suppose it makes any difference where you go. I don't care - as far as I'm concerned, when you die that's it! If there's anything after it'll take care of itself won't it?

ANDREA: Well it hasn't with you has it?

MATTHEW: Well it will when I eventually die, but since I haven't reached that spot yet, I've got some little time to wait no doubt.

ANDREA: Are you married?

MATTHEW: No, not now, she died. Lungs gave in. She suffered then she died and then that's it. I haven't seen her again - appearing out of nowhere! If she was still around no doubt she would have done - but she hasn't!

ANDREA: Well maybe she was on a different frequency from yourself.

MATTHEW: The way you're talking you'd think everybody was built like a radio set!

ANDREA: That's it! The most sensible thing you've said -

MATTHEW: Rubbish! Don't have any knobs and levers sticking out of your head! How do you tune it then? Where's your little cat's whisker - answer me that then!

ANDREA: Ask the social worker - he'll tell you.

MATTHEW: He hasn't got too much to say - 'How are you enjoying life?' he will say - 'Not much I expect.' Quite right! The only sensible thing the fellow ever says. 'Just part of the Medical Practioner's ideas of keeping in touch with every-one - see if they're all right!'

ANDREA: Don't you like him?

MATTHEW: He's all right. Pops in once in a while when he's in the area doing his good deeds! His idea for me to just sit here and relax - think of clouds scudding across the skies, or waving palm trees or sea rolling up a beach!

ANDREA: How old are you?

MATTHEW: Why? I don't think it's of any relevance to you whatever! You're a ghost and you need help. The vicar will probably disperse you into nothing - you're just someone's vague conscious awareness, I suppose rambling about nothing!

ANDREA: Well it's interesting that you think that kind of thing is possible!

MATTHEW: I don't think it's possible at all! It's the ramblings of these Spiritualist people - talking about life after death and your consciousness continuing - a load of rubbish! No proof at all!

ANDREA: Can you prove it is nineteen fifty three?

MATTHEW: Of course I can. It's on the newspapers as clear as a bell.

ANDREA: They are just a figment of your imagination.

MATTHEW: How can they be! You're the figment. That's probably what you are! You aren't a ghost really - you're just in my imagination! I must have eaten something that didn't agree with me!

ANDREA: When did you retire?

MATTHEW: Oh not that long ago. Chest been playing me up, couldn't breathe, couldn't work then after that. It's only a matter of well......half a dozen months...I don't know, wasn't much more than that......July it was I think.

ANDREA: You know it's an interesting situation - you who died in nineteen fifty three, and me, alive in nineteen eighty eight, and we are able to sit here and converse!

MATTHEW: I don't know why you don't go! There is no point in you telling me all this absolute rubbish - trying to make me believe, for some God forsaken reason -these stories!

ANDREA: I want you to wake up to your real situation, because you are holding yourself back. When people die, all they do is move away from the physical body - because that is what has really died, the body. The person then has a different kind of body, it is a lighter body and it doesn't suffer all the problems the physical had. The imagination is very strong due to habit patterns, and some people, like yourself, get trapped into believing that they are still in their existence. Really, if you observe things - and you can - you must KNOW you are not in that life any more - you KNOW you are not.

MATTHEW: Haven't you got a message from my mother then? Something important? From my grandfather or Aunt Lucy - anything you want! Now listen here, you whatever you are, I've been on this earth for the best part of about sixty three years, and you aren't telling me that everything is a fragment of my imagination - because it hasn't happened! I haven't separated from my body and carried on living in a world of my own or whatever it was! No, I'm still here and I'm still doing what I've done, and I worked a lot of those years.

Eight of them taken away for the country and I come back and everything's in disorder! Then I work, then I finish, and then I've a right to sit down and relax and do anything I like - without interference from.......apparitions! I don't think there's any point in you bothering to stay here. I don't know why you don't just dis-apparition or whatever you call it and take yourself somewhere else. I'm not interested in anything you've got to say. I'll have a word with that social worker when he comes.....and the vicar.

ANDREA: Well why not think about your life and the purpose of it.

MATTHEW: Listen I went to church when I was a child. I was christened, baptised and confirmed. What more do you want?

ANDREA: Well are you in Heaven now?

MATTHEW: I'm not dead either! We talk about life, of course we do, over dominoes. Yes we reminisce. Oh yes we get older and one day we will die and that will be it. When your time comes you have no control over it, and if there's a God in Heaven, he'll take care of us. So there is no point in wondering about our lives because it's not in our control. Just go away! I'm not interested! Go and haunt somewhere else!

Uriel reappeared - Alan was sitting up straight again.

ANDREA: Sorry about that! I couldn't do much for him I'm afraid!

URIEL: Well that's the way things are. I think you will have found the difficulties of the problem. It certainly does emphasise the fact that you just can't go up to someone and say 'Hi there, you are dead! Would you like to change your ways, listen to what I've got to say?' No, I'm afraid it just doesn't work like that.

ANDREA: Well you can't think of anything to PROVE anything!

URIEL: Exactly the point, you see. This is what I've said to people on earth. You might as well try to sort your problems out whilst you are there, and aware of them. You can do something about them, whereas the moment you are discarnate again, you are not really in a position to think for yourself on some occasions.

You now know the difficulties of the very many people who donate a vast amount of their existence to trying to sort these people out. No wonder people stay like it for centuries of your time!

ANDREA: I hope I haven't queered your pitch!

URIEL: Oh no! Of course we will go down again. Angelo will go in his dog-collar, and myself as the merry social worker. What is happening for this fellow is that he is virtually reliving a small cycle of three or four days, all of the time. It is a bit awkward. No doubt he'll tell us about this experience.

ANDREA: You know I can't blame him for thinking I

needed exorcising! What if he heard a current news bulletin on our radio? What could he put that down to?

URIEL: That's always supposing that he could hear it.

ANDREA: Well he heard me.

URIEL: He had been attuned of course. He may well catch a certain influence from a radio, but it doesn't mean he will give it credence because it isn't coming from anywhere. Its just so many random thoughts.

ANDREA: What are the mechanics of it? You told him to sit in his chair and think of something pleasant. Relax and then what?

URIEL: It is this condition of total relaxation he needs and then we have to get hold of him in that condition and attune the mind to a state of inertia, so to speak and then bringing his thoughts so that he is aware of you. It is a case of introducing you into his thought patterns, because for him of course you don't exist. The only way we exist is to relate entirely with the situation he is in.

No doubt the things you've said to him will put him in a fluster, and make him think. He is his own worst enemy of course. He is not in any way an evil person, neither is he particularly good, a little selfish, but as you said yourself, a little closed-minded and won't accept, and I do think that when he does discover it, he will be pleasantly surprised.

ANDREA: What did he die of, by the way?

URIEL: He died during a violent fit of coughing.

MATTHEW PART TWO

(Six months later, we were sitting but I did not know who would come through)

MATTHEW: You again!

ANDREA: Hello, Matthew.

MATTHEW: Yes......it IS you isn't it?

ANDREA: It is.

MATTHEW: Well, what have you come for this time?

ANDREA: I just thought you'd like a little chat.

MATTHEW: What about - ghosts or the time of day?

ANDREA: It depends what you think IS the time of day!

MATTHEW: It's important that isn't it?

ANDREA: It is to you.

MATTHEW: No. I mean to everyone...what they think is the time of day. Because....people would think I was absolutely potty talking to you! But, since you last appeared, I've been thinking. Habits are very easy and very strong aren't they?

ANDREA: They certainly are!

MATTHEW:Is it really nineteen eighty something?

ANDREA: Eighty eight - yes, it is.

MATTHEW: You ought to speak to my...visitor.

ANDREA: Why?

MATTHEW: Oh, he talks very similar things. Said he thinks time isn't important. Is it important to you that it's nineteen eighty eight?

ANDREA: No, not really. It's just a point of reference isn't it?

MATTHEW: You mean that it's just somewhere to start or finish? Oh, how do you do it by the way?

ANDREA: Do what?

MATTHEW: Appear.

ANDREA: It's something that someone manages to fix up. Am I just a blur, Matthew?

MATTHEW: No.....you're a little clearer, I suppose. If time isn't important...time has passed by and I've been looking at things from a fixed reference point, how can you go through life without time? If it's not important, how do you fix your ideas?

ANDREA: Time is a sequence of events. Time as it is known puts some order in Society, doesn't it?

MATTHEW: Yes but....you said last time it wasn't you that was the ghost - you LOOK like a ghost to me. Ghosts are

105

often dead, yet if it's nineteen eighty eight to you and to me it's been nineteen fifty three, it presumes you've continued thinking about time from your demise - doesn't it?

ANDREA: Well it would do if I had demised, from that point of view that you're talking of, but you're the one that's demised.

MATTHEW: That's the point, if you've continued and I haven't, therefore it's me that's demised and you haven't. Therefore I've stopped living but... didn't... hm.. some fellow say...hm some philosopher...that was it Descartes! I used to read a lot. Didn't he say 'I think therefore I am'?

ANDREA: That's right, he did.

MATTHEW: I'm still thinking.

ANDREA: Oh, I haven't said you've stopped existing! I just said you've stopped living on the earth - you've demised from this particular point where time is more important.

MATTHEW: You see, since you last called, I've been thinking. If I had ceased living according to the natural order of time, presumably I've demised. What about my social visitor - he seems alive to me?

ANDREA: He IS alive to you.

MATTHEW: Well if I'm demised shouldn't he be as well?

ANDREA: Well he is! He is compared to me, in relationship to me. You see it is possible for many people to exist at the same time on different levels. Parallel existence.

MATTHEW: Why didn't I know?

ANDREA: Why didn't you know what?

MATTHEW: That I'm dead?

ANDREA: You did know but you refused to accept it because it wasn't what you expected. You must have been aware of your own funeral and all of the things that happened after you died in your coughing fit. Your mind wouldn't allow you to accept it.

MATTHEW: Why have things continued then?

ANDREA: Because you wanted them to - in your mind.

MATTHEW: Do you mean that....provided you think a thing, it will be?

ANDREA: Well that's what you just said 'I think therefore I am' - or rather Descartes said, but nature abhors a vacuum - you just cannot have a void, so you fill the void with something.

MATTHEW: But surely!....I never considered dying for one moment...because of that, I never expected it to happen - I expected things to continue. Presumably that was the reason - if you think of things strongly enough and...

ANDREA: This is the trouble with habit patterns, you see. They become grooved in the mind and you just carry them on.

MATTHEW: Why didn't I read about it in the paper? About the Queen's son, for instance, growing up?

ANDREA: Well you weren't able to imagine things in the paper that you didn't know had happened. Your newspapers would contain just what you expected them to contain. Your imagination would not stretch as far as the Queen's children growing up.

MATTHEW: How long are you stopping?

ANDREA: As long as you want.

MATTHEW: You don't want a cup of tea, do you?

ANDREA: No, thank you very much, I've just had one. You know you really don't even need to drink tea now.

MATTHEW: I need a drink to sort this lot out! I had the other young fellow come the other day....disreputable devil he was!

ANDREA: Why?

MATTHEW: Oh it's just the policy of modern youth, I imagine. You fight for your country and what do you get - layabouts! Anyway, he also said 'you are what you are'. Well, I knew what he was!

ANDREA: What was he ?

MATTHEW: Oh a friend of the social worker's I think. He sounded like he was probably one of his cases. He said 'You are what you are - if you want to be an old misery - well, you are an old misery'. I said 'Well I imagine you are what YOU are - you're a layabout, you are what you are!' but he's a nice enough fellow, he didn't take offence, he'd got something about him. 'That's right' he said, 'if I was a layabout, then that is what I would be, but I could change it, I could become a social worker. Now a grumpy old devil...what can he become?' Then he left. He didn't eat anything either.

ANDREA: Didn't need to you see. Like your pipe - it's just a habit pattern.

MATTHEW: The wife bought it for me. I wonder where she is? Likely to be around somewhere if she's suffered the same fate.

ANDREA: It all depends on her state of mind.

MATTHEW: Is that what it's all about? What's the point? The point of it all, the point of you?

ANDREA: Well as I told you, I am on the earth. I've come to have certain experiences that will teach me about myself.

MATTHEW: If you're on the earth being a ghost, where am I?

ANDREA: You're just off the earth being a ghost. Sort of trapped really. You are not going backwards and you're not going forwards - you're not doing anything.

MATTHEW: If I was to walk out of the door....why aren't I fifty years older, by the way?

ANDREA: It's all in the mind isn't it? What is age?

MATTHEW: So when my perspective of time finished, I didn't age?

ANDREA: No, in fact you could go back to feeling just how you felt in your prime of life.

MATTHEW: If I was to go out of the door and walk down the street, if it is all in my mind, everything should be as it was.

ANDREA: Everything would be just what your mind wants it to be. No doubt just what you can remember. If you can think over the things I've said, and perhaps accept them, you are stretching your mind - opening it. All life, wherever you are, depends on just what you allow yourself to believe, to feel, to see and to experience....

MATTHEW: Well, it is an experience talking to you. You're not at all bad for a ghost. I imagine one can get quite...er, get used to you. How does Heaven fit into all of this?

ANDREA: It's just a state of mind. It doesn't exist as a place.

MATTHEW: Um....what do I expect to find outside my memory?

ANDREA: You really have to look at what you have now - and see the reality of it. Don't expect - just experience. It must be difficult shaking off almost seventy years of habit patterns, but if you realise there is something not quite right, and ask someone for a little help, then there is a lot more to find and be interested in.

MATTHEW: Well if I live here in this pleasant little house, the way I've always done, what will I have if I go looking?

ANDREA: Well, as you know, what you have doesn't amount to much, really. What are you doing with your life? You have no health problems now to prevent your doing anything you want, anything you are interested in that you didn't do in your earth life. Just test yourself and see what you are capable of - you will be surprised I think. You have total freedom and you are allowing yourself to be trapped in old routines and memories.

MATTHEW: If I were to walk out of that door today, lock it, walk away, never to come back....what will that do?

ANDREA: Well....that would be marvellous, for that would unshackle you. If you said to your social worker or his friend 'Show me something else, show me what I haven't got,' you would really be amazed.

MATTHEW: Hm......Are you going?

ANDREA: Does it look as though I'm going?

MATTHEW: Yes, you're fading away a bit. Hm....very strange...hm...well maybe see you again sometime.

ANDREA: Oh I hope so.

MATTHEW: Perhaps you should have haunted me earlier.

JACK

JACK: Good evening. Very nice to be here I'm sure. Well things have come to a pretty pass, haven't they?

ANDREA: Have they?

JACK: Oh yes they have. I'd never have thought of doing this at one time - never have thought it at all. Now, after all this time that I've been told to keep my mouth shut, I've got to come up and say summat. Doesn't make sense does it? You go to them queer churches down the road. You've got to learn to be spiritual. They come along and tell you all sorts of things. They bring your relatives to you, that's gone and in Heaven. And here I am, I'm no more in Heaven than the cat next door - and I'm not your relative. So it's come to a pretty pass hasn't it? It's all wrong.

ANDREA: Is it? Don't you like it?

JACK: I haven't done it long enough to see if I like it. Things aren't what you're told - and that's the truth. You go through life and you don't know what's happening from one day to the next. You work, it's a struggle to try and save a bit - then what happens? You snuff it and then, when you get here, you find it's all been wrong and a waste of time. There I was sat on me chair with me feet in front on the cat. I'd just put me pipe out and I was minding my own business, nodding off. The wife was knitting. Then there was a tap on the shoulder and I said. 'Who the hell are you?' He says 'Come on Jack, let's go.'

'Let's go where? What're you doing in my house, anyway?'

'It ain't your house anymore, Jack,' he says.

'Who are you, Corporation or summat?' I says.

'Look round Jack, have a good look at your missus.'

And there she's knitting away and there's me watching her. I thought I was watching her anyway, and then I realised I was sat in the chair an'all. 'My God' I says, 'What's happening -that's me there!'

'Was you Jack' he says.

'Who the hell are you anyway?'

'Don't you remember me?'

Then I looked back fifty years ago! Harvey it was. He got killed out in Africa. I hadn't seen him since we were lads together.

'Come away lad' he said, 'Time we went.'

'I can't go just like that! What's happening here?'

'Nowt you can do lad,' he says, 'Come away.'

So I sort of shrugged and went with him.

ANDREA: Did you realise that you'd died?

JACK: Not a lot of choice in it when I'm there, sat by t'fire and I'm watching meself and he's telling me to come away. Knew damn well I was dead - well sort of. Di'n't sort of sink in real quick, 'cos I was asking him all sorts of questions. 'What's going on Harvey?'

'Look Jack' he says, 'You're dead.'

'What!' I said, 'How can I be dead? No good telling me things like that! YOU'RE dead - musta been dead fifty odd years! I must be dreaming!'

'Aye lad, you are,' he says, 'but you waint wake up.'

I turned round and looked back, and I was still sitting there, and the missus just knitting away. 'It's not real, Harvey, I can't be dead. I'm dreamin' - it must ha' been that cheese and onion we had for tea!'

'Ti'n't that lad, ti'n't that. Come away, I want to show you summat.'

So I went off wi' him. Nowt else to do was there?

ANDREA: Did you feel all right?

JACK: I felt all right but things didn't look right - as if I'd had a few too many. But I wasn't a drinking man meself - didn't drink an awful lot. Anyway, we went into street and he says,

'Look, look at this lot' he says.'Jack, you see it? Well say goodbye to it cos that's it - gone.'

'What're you talking about Harvey? It i'n't gone - it's still here.'

'Well,' he says, 'it won't be here much longer.'

Then I felt sort of giddy and I thought I was falling. Then things looked different. I was told later on that that was when I really died - passed away. Up to that point I was still teetering on the brink, but then that wur it. I couldn't do nowt about that, it was over with. I couldn't go back if I wanted to.

ANDREA: So when you felt a bit giddy - that's when you actually died?

JACK: Aye. When I turned round things weren't the same. There wur a street there right enough but it wa'n't the street I was used ter. There was plenty of folk about.

'It's your new home,' he says. 'Just to help you settle down, get your bearings at first and see how things go from there. It's not where you're going to end up Jack, so don't worry about it. In a while someone'll come along and have a word with you - to help you along a bit. I've done my bit and I'm off now. I've got other things to do. It's been nice seeing you Jack. Don't worry about folks around here, they won't bother you.'

'But Harvey,' I said, 'there's all sorts o' things I need to know - what's going on? Don't just go clearing off like that - what am I supposed to do? I don't know anybody around here.'

He says 'You will Jack, you will.'

And then he sort of disappeared - he went. I lit my pipe and looked about me. The place needed a lick of paint, but di'n't look too bad. It wur a strange sort of dream - then I thought 'What if it i'n't a dream and I don't wake up? Then there was a tap on door. Well I'd sat on this seat in this hall like, when a fellow came in.

'Now then Jack,' he says. I looked him up and down. He seemed an ordinary sort of chap.

'I've come to help you along,' he says. 'To explain a few things. This isn't a dream you're having. You really have died. It will take a while for you to get used to it, because it's totally different to what you expected. I know that. Anyway, my name's Eric and I've come to give you a hand, just to explain one or two things.'

Why I asked him to sit down and tek his ease. I said 'I'd offer you a drink, but I haven't got anything in. I haven't got any money. I haven't got anything. Pension's due of course on Thursday, so we should be all right then.'

112

'Jack' he says, 'you won't be getting any pension on Thursday.'

'Well how am I supposed to live? Got to rely on that coming in!'

'You don't need money, Jack.'

'Don't need money! What sort of place is this? Not Communist is it?'

'No, no Jack' he says. 'It's going to take a little while for you to know what's going on, for you've a lot of fixed ideas in your mind. Things you've always lived by. Now for instance that lot who ran the country that you always felt a lot about! Well you don't have to worry about them any more. We don't have that sort of thing here.'

'How are we going to manage without that - who does the governing around here then - who tells you what to do?'

'Why no one' he says. 'We give you a few guidelines, tell you the sort of things you've got to keep your eye on, and then you do it yourself. You know what you're doing.'

'Why' I says, 'that's all very well -'

'Now look here Jack,' he says,'first of all get yourself organised. Get out and meet people hereabouts. They're the same as you, they're no different. You might even know one or two of them. I'll come back tomorrow. Try thinking about yourself a bit. You know how you used to when you were sat in front of the fire. Reminisce like you used to. Life goes on and you've to think about what you've had before you can go any further. This isn't the end but you need to sort yourself out a bit. To be honest with you Jack - I feel that I can be...'

Like a fool I said 'Oh you can be Eric. I like people ter be straight up wi' me.'

'Well' he said, 'you're a miserable old sod!'

Well that took me aback a bit, cos nobody's ever said that to me before.

'Be honest with yourself, Jack. Anyway, I'll leave you alone for a bit. You'll find plenty of food in the larder, and whatever you want, just think about it and it'll be there. I'll just show you one or two folk in the street and I'll be off. I'll be back tomorrow to have a chat with you, and a walk round.

113

There's a park over yonder if you feel like a stroll.'

So we went for a walk - I felt quite fit really - I hadn't walked for quite a while, used to get short of breath. I was expecting to feel a bit shaky on my pins but I di'n't. He introduced me to one or two people. Had sandwiches and a drink with them. I di'n't think too much of one chap, thought him a bit common.

'That's no way to think Jack! We're the same sort, you and me. You're no better than me! I'm no more common than you are!'

That took me back a bit. I wondered what was going on.

'Your thoughts, Jack. You can't hide 'em. We're all similar types here you'll find - we all had the same type of lives. That's why we're all living in the same area.'

'Why I don't think I'm like you' I said.

'You are Jack, you are.'

ANDREA: Didn't you like him?

JACK: Well he was a real nosey bugger!

'Anyway' he says, 'it's not going to make us enemies. Gonna be friends Jack. You'll find they keep coming round asking if you've been thinking about yourself. I don't know why they do that - I've been here about three Christmases, and they still ask.'

'Oh, you have Christmas over here?' I said

'Oh aye. It's no different really in some things.'

The following day Eric came back and I said to him 'What religion are you then?'

'I haven't any religion. That's all behind you. You don't have religions around here. There's a church if you want to go to it, but you don't have to. What I want to show you Jack is that things can be really different - you don't have to stop here. You can move on to something better. You've just got to realise a few things about yourself. That deep inside you there's something better than what you are.'

'Well, I don't think there's out wrong wi' me. I'm fine enough. I don't interfere with anybody and I hope they won't interfere with me.'

'Well that isn't quite right you know - still have it your way and I'll keep coming to see you from time to time, and bring along friends who've been like you, to have a chat. You're new yet and things are different for you.'

'I feel a bit different in meself you know. Feel as though I could run miles.'

'Well' he said, 'go ahead - go and run miles.'

'Probably kill me!' I took out me pipe. 'Them down there say you keep coming round asking them to change. Change what? There's nothing for me to change. I'm alright as I am.'

'Well,' he said, 'you don't have to smoke for a start.'

'What!' I said. 'I like me pipe!'

'Well I know, but do you need it Jack? What is it? It's only just to suck on isn't it? Why don't you put your thumb in your mouth?'

'Well that's not very dignified is it? Can't walk around with my thumb in my mouth all day!'

'What's the difference?' he said.

'Well you're being childish. If that's what you've come to talk about you might as well not bother!'

'All right Jack, I'll leave you to it. If you want me just think about it.'

And then he went. I waved to that nosey old....beggar across the road. Real aspidistra-faced she is, you know. Always peering out of the curtains seeing what's going on. Her house is shabby, could do with some new curtains as well!

Well that wur it really. Went on like that for a while. It got a bit tedious in time for I hated him down the road. He was really nosey, interfering, overbearing - and what with her across road watching my every move! Then he kept saying 'You're the same as us Jack! That's why we all enjoy being together - because we're all alike!' I wa'n't like him at all. I soon got to dislike it round there. I got used to the idea that I couldn't go back to my old life, but I said to Eric one day,

'Can you get me on transfer list and get me a move out of here, 'cos I want a different street. I'm not really happy here.'

115

'Well' he said, 'I wish I could do that Jack, but I can't. You see when you were working on earth -'

'Oh aye, I remember, in saw mill.'

'No Jack, not in the saw mill, and we don't want to hear about all that dust and stuff you got on your chest, that put you out of gear for six months. No. It's a case of all you were doing. All that, brick by brick, built this here place, on this land, right next to that lot, because you really are like them Jack - you're the same. You were always an interfering individual, always telling people how to do things, weren't you? Be honest.'

Well I suppose I did use ter put people ter rights - tell 'em ter ger on wi' it - straighten their lives out and stop whimpering all over the place. I'd been through a war fer them! I used ter tell 'em an' all - while you lot are prancing around like a lot o' nancies - I've been through a war fer you. Was it worth it? No it wa'n't! Not fer people like them! Now there's this Eric telling me summat I di'n't want ter believe.

You see Jack, why you're disliking it here is because you're seeing in these people the worst parts of yourself..'

'Well that's it then i'n'it? I suppose this is called purgatory is it? Like this fer the rest of eternity! Well it's enough ter mek a man miserable to his soul!'

'You were Jack, you were a miserable old bugger, you know that. You never had a good word to say for out, but it doesn't have to stay like this Jack.'

'Oh aye, how do I get out of here - win Pools?'

'No, it doesn't rely on anything like that. It's just you Jack, what you'll do now in the next six months.'

'Next six months!' I nearly choked on me pipe. 'Don't want ter stop here another six months!'

'Might not take that long at all. But it's up to you to straighten yourself out. You've got to see you've got the same faults as them. Do what I asked you six months ago - think when you've done something that you shouldn't have done and admit to yourself that you were in the wrong.'

'Aye lad, I'll mebbe think about it. Yes, I'll think about it in a while.' I got me pipe out - well it didn't feel right shov-

116

ing me thumb in me mouth did it? Anyway he went after a drink and then I decided to go for a walk.

I passed the church on the way and I thought I'd go in there and see what it's like. You get a bit o' peace in churches. Nobody was there except an old lady sweeping up. I sat down near the front end. Then I got to thinking in the quiet.

That there Eric, he seems a nice enough young fellow. He hasn't done me any harm, and yet he tells me all these things. There's no reason for him to bother with me even. He's a bright young fellow, nothing seems to depress him much.......perhaps he's right. Perhaps it is sort of me that's at fault. Perhaps, sort of looking at it, yes I am sort of.......so really when you think about it, he might be right and I ought to do something about it. I used to raise my voice a bit when I didn't really have to.........

I felt a bit depressed really. It comes hard on a man at my age to sort of look at his self and think 'ow wrong he's been. I 'aven't recognised it of course - 'aven't been bothered about it. I just said owt really - what I felt wur right. Then when I think about our lads - I think well, aye, the missus of course, she never had a word of recrimination against me, but I knew it had been said somewhere that I'd driven lads away. One had joined Army and got his self killed. Aye that wur a bit of a blow, and t'other cleared off to Australia, I think it wur. Never heard from him agen. I don't know whether he's dead or alive.

It can't be all my fault, of course - no it can't be that. They wur just going the way they wanted. I used ter work hard in my life - that's the thing, you see. I used ter do what I thought wur best, to work hard, provide the comforts we needed and after all I did buy that new wireless so that Edna - that's the missus, could listen to all sorts of programmes on it when I wur out. She used to enjoy that a lot. She used ter say all sorts o' things when I came in - but I di'n't really want ter hear it of course - I wur too tired.

Well, I wanted ter see Eric the following day when I'd got up and got myself organised, but he di'n't come. So I went for a walk again. Wasn't much else ter do, you see. I di'n't

117

want ter listen to them trying ter be funny - telling the same old jokes over and over. I don't want ter be knowing about that kind o' thing at my age. They wur a bit on the crude side some o' them.

I ambled along just on t'side o' park, and I saw it wasn't a place I'd bothered much wi' before. It wur different. I had a look round pond, then I went over to a gate at yon side that I'd not seen before - and thur wur Eric! Must have been on his way to see me.

'Hello' I said.

'Made it then' he said.

'Well I wur just looking round. Going for a walk, clear the air a bit 'cos you hadn't come.'

'No' he said. 'I wasn't rushing because I was expecting to meet you here before now.'

'Well how'd you know I would be coming this way?'

'Why it's the only way for you to come.'

And that wur it, really. He says 'Come away, it's a bit different for you now.' We had a walk round and he showed me a few things of interest in the church - coffins and bits of brass rubbings, wur people had written on the walls long ago -and the choir stalls and such. Then we went back down street and had a cup of tea. Then he said, 'Right, well I'll be seeing you Jack. Things are going to be different.'

I thought what a nice lad he wur - always willing to spend time wi' me - not like most of the young uns. Used ter get me talking and thinking a lot. Never met anybody quite like him - he used ter tell me stories of things he'd done and places he'd seen. Done a lot for such a young lad really.

Anyway, next day I went out into street........it seemed quite different somehow. It seemed a bit brighter. Across road she'd got some new curtains and she'd had place painted up. In fact when I looked around the whole place seemed a lot brighter. Then across the road someone else came out and said 'Morning' and came across for time o' day. I thought t'other must of moved. Bye she went quick! Must have flitted overnight!

Then someone else came along to chat. Said I must be

new around there and I said 'No, you're new folk - I've been here about six months.' Then I thought to meself I didn't want to cause a bother with them being strangers.

Things had changed, the people wur different. It seemed as though I'd been moved sumhow - the same street but everybody moved out and new people in. Took a bit of getting used to that did. Nice lot of people though, a lot more encouraging they wur. So I used to go out and play Beetle and get involved wi' Whist Drive an' all! A lot nicer though, than it used ter be. In fact I enjoy people coming in now, fer a chat and a reminisce. Eric comes by about once a week. Everybody knows him and welcomes him along. Bit like a parish priest he is except that you don't look at him like that. He doesn't have a dog collar on! He's a friend really, someone you can rely on.

So that's it. That's what I've come ter say.

PART THREE

This part of the book tells of the experiences of six very different people, who were killed by other people.

The first four stories came as I sat at the keyboard, but the sixth, the Mercenary came one night as one of the most vivid dreams I have ever had. It was so real that I wondered if I was connected with it in some way. I certainly seemed to be seeing it and experiencing it from the prisoner's viewpoint!

Then, during the following morning, I felt that it was shown to me to include in this book.

Then comes Archie. Once again this is one of the experiences of a communicator through Alan's trance.

FRANK

I was brought up strictly. My parents were Italian American and they were good Catholics. They believed in family life and did their best to make us good Catholics too. There was a problem though. We were very, very poor and it was a struggle to live.

The more children my mother had, the poorer we became. Still they tried to teach us right from wrong and to be always polite - even if we couldn't read or write. School was a problem for my parents. It wasn't that there was no school for us, it was that we had no decent clothes to go in - so we didn't go. Our lives were a long game in the streets, in the gutters, raiding trash cans for scraps of food or anything else that took our fancy. Even my father was reduced to looking through trash to see if there was anything he could use in any way for the house.

The house consisted of three rooms and two upstairs. There were eleven of us living there at one stage. True that stage didn't last long because as the kids got to the age of ten or eleven, they left home.

120

They became vagrants, sleeping rough and, I am sorry to say, turning to crime. They had already belonged to gangs from the age of five - street gangs who stole from market stalls and then from each other. Gangs who fought like animals and became vicious and cruel. In the poor areas - the ghettos, you had to be tough to survive. Any weakness and you went under.

By 'went under' I really mean you got trodden under the many feet of the rival gangs in fights. I have often looked back at a battleground and seen an inert body lying there - never to get up again. The police could do nothing. No-one ever split on anyone else. They just closed ranks. This happened whatever and whoever was suspected by the police of anything. People were afraid to talk to the police in case they themselves were 'fingered'.

It was a harsh, violent life and I was no better than the others - except I wanted to be a cop.

I had this longing since I first saw a cop pulling someone's dog out of the river where it had been thrown in by a gang. They had tied a brick around its neck - it was only a tiny pup, and to teach the owner a lesson or other, they threw it in at a fairly fast-moving spot. The cop had seen them though and went after it.

The gang jeered when he brought it out, and the owner said he didn't want it any more. No doubt he thought it better for the dog and himself to let it go. The cop took the dog to his car and they drove off. I will never forget the look on that guy's face as he held the wet and frozen little animal to him, to pass some of his body warmth to it.

As this is not meant to be my life story - rather my death story, I will get down to business.

I had been a cop for twenty years. It had been a tough life - but I was tough. I had killed a lot of desperate men who had tried to kill me. I had arrested thousands of people - who, driven only by poverty, chose to live outside the laws of the country. I had had some very close shaves myself and had spent a lot of time being stitched up and having bullets dug out of me.

The night I came to talk about was a festival night for

some of the coloured population of my territory. We expected trouble and had put on our bullet shields under our vests. We had even been briefed by our station boss, because he must have smelt something in the air.

Well it turned out to be one of the biggest gang fights I have ever seen. We had help from outside the territory, outside our precinct, outside our county in the end. The fighting went on all through the night and into the next day.

My partner and I had been in at the beginning of course when we followed a group of coloureds creeping along a darkened street. We kept well back and even doused the lights of the car. Ahead we saw a house door open and a further group joined up making quite a big party.

We followed them to a festival area where there was a bonfire on a parking lot, with people selling ice-creams, hot dogs and other traditional foods. There was music and dancing and all was going well until this group arrived.

They barged their way in and we got out of the car having called for back up on the radio. We dare not go in yet and things were a bit quiet really - just a bit of grabbing of girls and joining in the dancing, a bit of stealing and demanding food for free. But of course there were too many of them for it to stay quiet, and soon, we saw approaching from another direction, another gang.

We radioed in again, just as the back up was approaching, and the rival gang hit the firelight.

Then all hell let loose. There were scuffles, screams, knives were out, bodies were dropping, carts were overturned, people were scattering in all directions to get away from the scene. We had just to watch for a while until a sergeant arrived to direct us - it was that big a fight.

Then we went in, guns in hand and the sergeant called out with a loud hailer for them to stop fighting. That was procedure and of course it did no good at all. We went in a line towards the main area of fighting. We had a small hand knife shield to try to keep the knives away from our bodies, but many of the cops thought them worse than useless and preferred to keep their other hand free.

On this occasion I had my shield and found I could ward off a few knives as I went in, the idea being to pull out anyone on the aggressive. I hauled one guy out with my gun hand, having first clouted the side of his head with the gun. I stuck my shield away and started to pull him out of the foray. Suddenly I felt a sharp pain from under my arm towards my chest and I looked down into the dark, beautiful Italian eyes of a young girl prostitute. As I felt myself going down, the world disappeared from my eyes. The noise went, the smells went - and I went.

I woke up it seemed at the time, stretched out on some bed in some very light and pleasant room. I wasn't able to get things together for a while and decided to get up and find out where I was. There wasn't a soul about the place so I wandered outside where there was a very green garden.

Everywhere was green in all its various shades. Very restful and calming I found it. In the middle of this garden was a fish pool with a seat alongside of it. I made for the seat and sat looking down into the depths of the pool. I had some thinking to do and I had always made for the river on my days off and enjoyed a bit of fishing. I was a slowish thinker and I was trying to fathom just where I was and how I had got there.

I then decided that I must have been dreaming. I did used to dream a lot - and in colour too. Some of the guys used to have nightmares but I was lucky, I guess, because I only had pleasant dreams like this one now. In my dreams a lot used to happen and so I just went along with this situation waiting for something to happen.

Imagine my surprise when a female appeared out of nowhere walking along towards my seat. Imagine my surprise when that female seemed very, very familiar to me.

She asked if she might sit down and I moved over for her. I noted her - dark, Italian eyes, slim and very lovely - where had I seen her before?

She began to speak and told me the strangest story. She said she had been used by a gang for prostitution. She was kept on drugs and spent her life fortunately in a haze. One night, she said, it was a special festival night and she and her pimps were out to see what was around for them, when a big fight began with two rival gangs.

This girl and her friends were high on booze and drugs and mixed up with it all, and, in the fight she pushed a long stiletto into a cop who was just taking out her protector. At this point in her story, she looked straight into my eyes and - I am amazed to tell you, I fainted right away! Everything went blank again!

The second time I came to my senses, I was sitting on the same seat in front of the same pool. This time seated by my side was a guy. I waited to see what he had to say. I had full memory of recent events, both what I had experienced and what the girl had told me sitting on this seat.

I felt something of the priest about the guy sitting with me. Then he asked me how I felt and I told him fine.

He then asked me if I knew I had been killed. I said I did. He then asked me if I was ready for work and I asked what kind of work.

'About the same as you've always done,' he said, 'helping people find themselves.'

'I've spent my life trying to keep, law and order,' I said.

'Yes, well, it has the same ending - they find themselves locked up and in the courts. Here we just want them to find themselves as being dead and no longer concerned with things of the earth.'

'Will you tell me why that young girl came along - was she dead too?'

'Yes she is. She came along because she is not really as bad as she seems. She is merely weak and when she is much stronger, she will be O.K. By coming to you and telling you that you died at her hands, she has greatly improved her lot. It took some doing, especially when you consider she has a lot to get out of her system - the drugs and the drink and things.'

'I am a bit confused still, you know. I don't think I am capable of helping anyone just yet.' I said.

'Well, there is no rush at all - take a vacation, do just what you want for a while and then we will see.'

I got up from the seat and walked off towards what I

assumed would be the town. I still had a lot of thinking to do. I wanted to get things sorted out. Then I turned around. He was still there.

'How can I get in touch with the young lady?' I asked. 'I might try to get sorted out with her, if that's O.K.'

'No problem at all,' he said, 'I'll take you along. It will not be as pleasant as this, but from time to time you can come along here, just as you used to do before when you went fishing.'

JACKIE

I was having a smashing time at the party. I hadn't wanted to come at first as Greg was not really the type I liked. Anyway I decided that as I hadn't anything else on that night, I would go along. Janice was pleased as she liked Greg's mate very much and preferred a twosome at parties - especially of the type this would no doubt turn out to be!

I got really done up - more than I did when I was keen really. I had got a nice frock from the catalogue - not paid for of course, but very nice all the same! Black with red trimming around the low neck and short hem. It really fitted where it touched as my mother used to say in disapproval when I wore anything like this.

Thinking of my mother, I realised just what fun life had become since I left home and moved in with Janice. We had blokes over to stay when we wanted - we did JUST what we wanted, when we wanted. Oh life was great, there's no doubt about that. What would my mother have said if she'd known I'd given up work for good?

Well, why work in a factory when you could get your money much easier, without getting up at dawn as well! I felt life was to be enjoyed - not to work like a donkey till you lost your looks and got old like my mother.

Janice came out of the bathroom in a nice dress she had got from the catalogue as well. Hers was blue, because that was her colour. She really looked good and I told her so.

'You don't look so bad yourself!' Janice had said.

We met the fellers in the pub, where it was very noisy and everyone seemed to be having a good laugh and joke as well as drink. I had my usual gin - people said it made you miserable, but it didn't me - it made me really giggly. After an hour or so we went off to the party.

Neither of us knew the girl who's place the party was at. It was at the other side of town and we had to have a taxi to get there. Greg started in the taxi, groping everywhere, but I stopped him as I didn't want my clothes getting all creased up. I saw that Janice was quite well gone already and they were getting up to all sorts opposite us. I told Greg to make do with watching!

It was a really good party, booze flowing like water, and I know Greg laced a couple of my drinks. We got up to everything there, once I'd had a few more. Then it happened. There was a big girl - you know big in front and she must have given Greg the 'come-on', because he went.

I couldn't believe it! One minute he was there and the next gone upstairs with this big woman. I felt really mad and decided I was off. I couldn't see Janice anywhere, so I got my coat and got out of the front door. I hadn't a clue what time it was. I hadn't a clue where I was - I would just get a taxi outside I thought. I was really upset.

Once outside, I started off along the pavement. It wasn't a main road, and, muzzy though I was, I knew I had to get to a main road if I wanted a taxi. On my right I saw a little snicket thing and at the other end I could see lights, so I thought that if I nipped through there, I would be on the main road in no time.

I was walking along this little alleyway and was almost at the other end, when I felt a hand come over my mouth, nearly choking me and then the next thing, a hot feeling in my chest - and then everything went dark.

When I came to I was in a lovely place. It wasn't a hospital - more like a very classy hotel. I seemed to be sharing a room with another girl of about the same age as me. Angela was her name.

Angela was a bit of a talker. She was worse than Janice and she could go. For a time I just sat there on this very nice lounger in this nice double room. I had a nice china cup of tea by me on a little table, and a plate of really nice chocolate biscuits. She must have known I had a sweet tooth.

It was only when Angela mentioned friends, that I started to remember that I had gone out with Janice somewhere. That was just where my memory stopped short. Where had we gone? Where was Janice? Where was I - come to that?

Then a bell went somewhere, and Angela said I was having a visitor, and she went to the door. I went on with my tea, and soon there was a knock on the door of the room. I shouted 'Come in' and in came my grandmother! I had such a shock I nearly dropped my cup.

Grannie sat down and asked if there was a cup for her. I got up and poured her out a cup of tea from the teapot on the tray on the sideboard, and brought it over. I was wondering if I was dreaming all this. I wondered if I had gone out somewhere and fainted or something. My Grannie had died four years ago, aged eighty - or near enough.

'Seventy five I was dear.' she said as if reading my thoughts.

'What's going on?' I asked her. I had always liked Grannie - I had got on better with her than with my mother. I felt Grannie had been a bit of a girl in her younger days - maybe a bit more like me in fact.

'You've been a bit of an idiot, girl' Grannie said. She always used to say 'girl', so this convinced me that this WAS in fact my Grannie. She took one of the chocolate biscuits and sipped her tea.

'You've got yourself killed, girl.' she said and then bit into her biscuit, as if she had told me about failing a school test.

I sat there thinking I must be going off my head and imagining the whole scene. I didn't say anything and neither did she. We just sat there.

Then I looked at her. 'You're not my Grannie, are you - because you're younger than Grannie. I've never seen my

Grannie look as young as you look!'

'It's being here that does that,' she said. 'Not that you'll get younger, because you're only twenty now - or were!'

'What do you mean -"were"?' I asked, still not knowing what was going on.

'Well, if you want me to spell it out, I will girl.' Grannie said. 'You and your friend went to a party after you'd visited a pub. You drank more than was good for you - stopped your being able to think straight. Then you got upset and walked off into the night on your own. You didn't realise it, but there was a very disturbed fellow hanging about that house you were in. He followed you and grabbed you in the alleyway you decided to go down. Unfortunately he stabbed and killed you. That is why you are here, and why I am here talking to you.'

Grannie looked deeply at me as she spoke and, at the same time I felt what I can only describe as a wall of warmth come all around me - like a very strong and comforting arm. I don't know what it was because there was too much to think about. It wasn't Grannie because she was holding her cup and saucer with two hands, and sitting there looking at me with her deep grey eyes.

I felt bad despite the 'arm'. I didn't know what to say. I couldn't really believe it but I knew that my Grannie had always been outspoken. She hated lies and always said that even if the truth hurts, you have to tell it. I remember her voice from the past saying this so often to my mother, when we were little.

Yet I couldn't be dead - murdered - stabbed. I didn't hurt. I had no wounds. I was fine. Was this the 'Life after Death' that they believed in at the Spooky Church? We had often gone in for a laugh and it couldn't have had anything to do with this, where I was now. I had never been in such a lovely place, with such lovely cups and furnishings. What was it all about?

'This is to help you understand it all,' Grannie said. 'Much better than to find yourself in some hospital or back street. You had enough of back streets in your life - short as it was.'

'But what have I done, Grannie, to die like this?'

'That is a question even I can't answer love. But, in time, and knowing you, it won't be that long, you'll know it all. You'll find the answers. In this place there is so much you will like and so much you can use. Soon you will know why. There is always a reason and you will find it - I promise you that!'

JOE

It was a long night it seemed to Joe. He walked around the perimeter of the yard again with Rex at his heels. It had been very quiet again and he thanked God he hadn't had to set the dog off after anyone. Rex was a friendly fellow with the two of them, but God help anyone who tried to get in the place!

Then he felt rather than saw Rex stiffen. He was at the halfway point of his round. Fred would be in the office now, and Joe was on his own here - 'Oh God, let's not have any problems!' he thought.

Rex looked up at him and Joe knew he wanted to be off the chain. He bent down and just as he was about to open the catch, something caught him a sharp blow on the back of his head. He went down as though pole axed. It seemed like seconds only after, that Joe found himself high up in the air above the compound, looking down on the whole scene. Rex had turned as Joe had gone down, but he too was hit very hard on the head with what looked to Joe, like a slab of stone. The dog crumpled up and Joe somehow saw the life force leave the inert body that was lying alongside his own.

There were three men, all masked and all in dark clothing, and they were making for the office where Fred and the keys were.

Without stopping to wonder what was happening to him Joe followed the men, who seemed totally unaware of his presence. One went round the front of the little building, where Joe could see Fred, just putting on the kettle. The man whistled and Fred looked up.

'Stay put Fred!' shouted Joe, but Fred was thinking it was him telling him it was time for their mug of tea. Joe knew that, as per their usual routine, Fred would make the tea and then come out to give him the double whistle signal that tea was ready. No doubt the men were waiting for Fred's leaving the protection of his locked office, to give that signal.

Joe felt totally helpless, he could do nothing. He thought strongly of Fred and found himself actually inside the office standing next to Fred and telling him not to go out, but to press the emergency button which would bring the police hot foot.

No matter what he did, Joe could not stop Fred's actions. He could just watch them and watch Fred walk into the trap. It happened the same way as it had for him. One of the three moved out of the shadows right up behind Fred and up came the heavy stone slab, and down went Fred. From then on it was all fast and silent. The men seemed to know just what they were after and how to get to it.

Joe stood looking down at Fred and realised he was still breathing. He wondered how he could get help for his mate. He felt so useless. He sat down in the office near the phone - each time he tried to press the button, his finger went right through the plastic. It was weird.

Then it struck him. He went back outside to where both he and Rex were lying. Both bodies were still - there was no rise and fall - no vitality as with Fred. 'Good God! What had happened to him?' his mind then blanked out and he knew no more.

ALEX

When I got out of my car, I had the feeling something was wrong, but I carried on in my usual way. I locked the garage door and walked to the side door of the house. My key was in the lock and I then heard a movement behind me. I felt a pain in the back of my head and that was the last I knew.

When I came round I was trussed up like a chicken in the kitchen. The door was open and there was a deathly quiet about the house. I wondered where Jane was. I wondered just what had happened and I tried to free myself but to no avail. I couldn't see too straight, so they must have hit me very hard, I thought. I decided to shuffle to the door and see what was going on. That was when I got the shock.

I found myself actually at the door, and for some reason, I turned back to where I had moved from. A shudder ran through me for my body was still there, tied up, on the floor and very still. I looked down at myself. It was like seeing double. My mind wanted to investigate this new problem, but I had to find out if Jane was all right. I left the kitchen and made for the living room. What a mess! Cupboards, drawers, shelves, all emptied. Furniture was tipped up and cushions gaping from the slashes from corner to corner. No Jane...no-one.

I tiptoed upstairs to find chaos everywhere, but still no Jane and no-one else. I looked at the bedroom clock, but it was gone, so I made my way back downstairs to the one in the cooker. It was then I realised that I had left work earlier that day, to go to the dentist. What a relief to realise that Jane would still be at the shop.

Instinctively I went to the phone, wondering if it would still be there. Miraculously it was, and I stretched out my hand to pick it up. It was then I discovered that, although I could see the phone, I was unable to pick it up or feel it. I wondered just how I could ring the police and Jane. As I thought of my wife, I seemed to feel her near and looked round. No, it must be my imagination. Then I thought of how she would feel when she saw all of this mess. What could I do?

Then I got a picture of her at the shop. She was having a tea break in the back room. I saw her in her overall, sitting at the table, a cup in her hand.

Jane! She appeared to jump as I mentally called her. Jane! Yes, she looked round at the door as if expecting me to walk in. So I moved to the door and as I did so, I realised that I was actually there, in the back room of the shop. I looked at Jane and saw she had gone a deathly white. She put the cup down and sat staring at me.

'Jane,' I said anxiously.

'Alex...' Jane fainted and fell to the floor. The chair went over, made a loud noise and Mrs. Brown came in from the shop.

'Are you all right Jane?' she asked. Then she saw Jane's body on the floor and called for help from the shop, going over to pick Jane up. Of course she was a dead weight and I started forward again as I had when Jane first started to fall. My hands couldn't make any kind of contact with anything. I just stood there helpless and unseen - that is apart from my wife Jane. I was sure she had seen me. That's why she had fainted.

I watched as Jane was revived with Mrs. Brown's smelling salts, she had told the junior to get from the first aid box.

'What happened, dear?' Mrs. Brown asked. I was amazed because I seemed to hear her also say, 'probably pregnant.'

Jane however hadn't heard her and was beginning to focus her eyes again. She didn't say anything to Mrs. Brown about what she might have seen. Instead she murmured something about feeling hot.

Mrs. Brown suggested that she rang me at work, and at that I looked at Jane and said 'I'm not there - I'm supposed to be at the dentist.'

Jane seemed to remember and told Mrs. Brown she would be O.K. The excitement subsided. Everyone went back to what they were doing before, so I sat down beside Jane, I didn't want to risk her seeing me opposite her again. I wasn't sure what I could do about anything. I really wanted to prevent Jane from getting the shock of seeing me at the house.

Then I thought of Jane's Auntie Ella. Although she was a bit of a dragon, the eldest of Jane's mother's sisters, I liked her and, more important still, she was a Spiritualist medium. The rest of the family laughed about this, but we all had to admit, her predictions did sometimes come about.

Once again, as I thought of Aunt Ella, there she was, or rather there I was. One minute I was there with Jane, and the next I was in Aunt Ella's flat.

She was sitting on a settee reading a paper. I stood in front of her a bit nervously for a while, not knowing what to do. Then, all of a sudden, she dropped the paper on to her knee and stared straight at me. 'Alex!' Aunt Ella did not look as fierce as usual, there was a nice soft glow about her. It encouraged me.

'I'm sorry, Aunt Ella,' I began. 'Can you help Jane?'

Aunt Ella didn't seem to hear me. She could see me, I know, but she just sat there staring. Then she spoke again. 'Alex! What am I seeing?'

'It's me all right. Can you hear me, Aunt Ella?' I smiled at her, pleased to be seen without causing distress. Even though she seemed not to hear me, I asked her to ring Jane. I told her the house was burgled. I repeated this several times but still she did not hear me.

Then all of a sudden she went to the telephone and dialled Jane's mother's number. No reply. I could see Jane's mother's house and it was all locked up, she was out. After thinking a bit Aunt Ella got out the directory and looked up the shop. Then she dialled the number.

Eventually Jane came to the phone and I wondered just what Aunt Ella would say. Once again I found I could be in two places at once. I saw Jane pick up the phone.

She was feeling a bit anxious because of her recent experience and because of her fainting - and now this phone call. She was worried what Mrs. Brown would be thinking. Strange how I could know all of these thoughts of people. I found myself going off into a deep thought about my own state, then I realised that I was missing the conversation. I refocussed.

Aunt Ella had asked if I was all right. Jane had said I was and why. Aunt Ella said she had had the strangest feeling that she had seen me very clearly. Jane asked what that meant if she had. I tried to put my arm around Jane because I could see her starting to feel ill again. I thought very hard 'Be strong, Jane'.

The strangest thing was that I saw a bright patch of blue

133

mist go around Jane and she stood straight again. I realised that my thoughts acted more than my words or appearance.

I heard Aunt Ella say she would go over to the house and see if I was all right. Jane wondered if I'd had a bad session at the dentist and said that she would be very grateful if Aunt Ella would go. So would I.

I got on the bus alongside Aunt Ella, sat beside her and tried hard to put my thoughts into her mind. It was difficult because she had started to worry about all the things that could have gone wrong in the dentist's chair. I waited for a gap. Eventually, as she walked up the garden path, I was able to hear her thoughts. 'I wonder if the house is all right? I wonder if he's had a heart attack?'

She found the side door unlocked and went in.

Of course, there was a great deal of hue and cry. Police, forensics, witnesses, courts, newspapers, finally a trial. Three men got a long imprisonment. Jane went through a bad time. Her family and friends were very supportive, but it took months for her to recover.

I tried many, many times to contact her in various ways. I did not want her to re-experience the shock of a full view of me, so I eventually gave up and settled for trying to comfort her, and help her cope with her life.

In time she got over the whole sad business and went back to work on a part-time basis. I would try again to contact her in the future, and in the meantime there were plenty of things for me to find out about 'life after death'.

ARCHIE

Archie was born in a very poor area of Chicago in the nineteen twenties. His mother never recovered from his birth, and she died when he was about a year old. His father did his best, but that consisted of leaving him to his own resources most of the time, so Archie grew up on the streets with the rest of the kids.

Archie was a bit of a slow thinker - he wasn't stupid, but

134

he had to really take time to digest what people said to him. As a result he was treated as though he was not quite right in the head. When he was old enough to look for work - all he managed to get was the sweeping up jobs in factories.

His work mates nicknamed him 'Stanley'. This was because of his slowness - they were cruelly likening him to the Stanley knife, which of course is very sharp indeed! Archie accepted this with his usual placidness, and just got on with his job.

Sadly, whenever things went wrong in the factories, and this was often, everyone put the blame on 'Stanley', so he got the sack. He got the sack so many times, that he never ever got beyond the job of odd-job guy.

People had no time for Archie, so he made no friends at all - apart from some pigeons and a small house mouse that he fed whenever he ate himself. He lived a lonely life in a tiny apartment in a very poor district. He made a very low income and could just make ends meet.

One night, coming back from his weekly shopping, he was mugged, knifed, robbed of the few cents he had, and left to drag himself up to his apartment, where he collapsed and died.

When he came to himself, he was in a strange town, sitting on a bench surrounded by pigeons, all pecking at the ground around him. They seemed quite tame when he talked to them, and Archie spent some time making friends with them. Then, in his placid way, he thought he had better find out where he was and how he had got there.

Soon, he saw approaching him, a cop. The cop had a pleasant face, and Archie decided that this was the guy to talk to.

Jack Daniels had indeed a pleasant face and was exactly what Archie needed at that time. He took Archie off to a coffee bar, gave him a coffee, and told him exactly what had happened to him. Archie seemed to accept all that Jack told him and was amazed when the cop then suggested they had a game of pool. No-one had ever wanted to play pool with Archie before - he had always pushed the balls around on his own. Not much fun - but better than passing the time staring at a mouse!

The rest of the guys in the pool hall were friendly and so

Archie experienced a whole new life. He walked about the town and found people sociable. It was an interesting place and he enjoyed watching and listening to people without feeling threatened. For a while he enjoyed the freedom and atmosphere of the place - then it began to pall on him. He was a creature of habit, and no matter how terrible and monotonous his work had been, he missed it. No matter how cruel and at times vicious his work mates, he missed the contact with them.

Then he wondered just where he was going to live, and how, and soon worked himself into a really worried state of mind. He went off to find the cop, Jack Daniels.

He didn't have to look far, for in fact Jack was expecting Archie's reaction, and was waiting for him on a nearby street corner.

Listening to Archie's worries, Jack soon got him fixed up with a nice apartment in a small block, with pleasant gardens and surroundings.

Although he accepted that he had died, Archie found it very difficult to accept his new life. There were things he could not tell the cop - no matter how friendly, a cop was still a cop, and Archie had never felt comfortable with them in his life. He stood in the yard of his apartment block feeling a bit low, when he saw a female in the next block's yard. He took courage in both his hands and called out'

'Hi...how ya doing?'

This is where Archie developed a friendship - perhaps the first in his life. The strange thing though, is that this friendship was one between two totally different worlds. Somehow the spirit communicators who regularly used Alan's trance mediumship, had linked Archie up with me. I was the female Archie 'saw' in the next yard.

I'd had no previous warning of what was happening, just the usual message into my head that 'someone' wanted to communicate. Alan and I had sat in the little room where we held these sittings. I put on the music and Alan went off into his relaxed state. I too was relaxing as I listened to the pleasant music. It seemed to take a little while for the communicators to get through, but eventually this very nasal American voice called out 'Hi...how ya doing?'

I soon got into chatting with Archie. He told me his story and how he was always called Stanley at work - I determined never to call him that. My maternal sympathy was strongly aroused for this guy who seemed to have had such a raw deal in life. Archie soon became my favourite, I felt some kind of affinity with him, and I had many talks with him.

I never ever found him 'slow'. In fact I discovered he had a very keen wit and he even told me he wrote poetry at times.

I discussed his problems with him and he always went away to think things over. I knew he was being helped by Jack Daniels and others on his side of life, he had to somehow shake off a very deprived life which limited him in all directions. No-one had ever wanted him. He had tried to enlist in the army at the beginning of the war, but had been turned down. He owned nothing. He existed with just the bare necessities of life. No-one gave him time - he had no-one to turn to with his problems. No-one liked him or bothered with him. What a lot of inhibitions to be brought up, understood and disposed of!

When I realised that Archie was bored with nothing to occupy him, I asked him what he would choose if he could do whatever he wanted. His reply was that he would keep chickens. I suggested he found Jack Daniels and asked for his help in this direction.

The next time Archie communicated, he had a small house at the side of a road, with a bit of land and some chickens. He was happy, but to be safe, he used to put a chair up against the door handle at night when he went to bed!

There were a lot of people going up and down this road Archie told me, so he put out a table and some chairs, and made people drinks - coffee or juices, if they wanted to stop and talk. Archie enjoyed the many conversations he had this way.

Then I suggested he took up another hobby, so he started oil painting. He painted pictures of chickens and gave them to people when they stopped for coffee! He of course still had problems to sort out. One deep set one was his reluctance to go far from his lovely little home - just in case someone else might move in! Another was that people who stopped off for a drink with him, often left things behind when they went.

These were personal possessions - cameras etc. and Archie was really worried that he might be accused of theft or receiving. So he laboriously wrote out lists and notices of what had been left, and stuck these up outside his house.

Eventually one of those helping him told him that when people had grown out of things - possessions - they just left them behind, and anyone else who might want them could have them. Just like children grow out of toys - they don't care who has them. So Archie was very happy to be able to give away these items.

The story of Archie is still going on. From time to time he will be linked up and we will have a chat. Naturally, I asked him where he sees me and what I look like. I must say these questions make him think I am a bit of a nut! Once it seems, we were in some cafe, having a drink and a chat. I told him that only he could see me - the other people in there couldn't. He found this very hard to accept and wondered what the people must think of him, talking to himself!

Eventually I told him that I was living in England, in a physical life. This time he decided that I really did have a problem and told me straight out that he was 'no shrink!' Each visit he would ask the same thing. 'D'ya still think you're living in England?'

Archie has now left his chicken farm. He has made a lot of discoveries about himself and moved on. He still comes along for a chat, but I can tell that the personality of Archie is getting looser. He is taking more interest in the realities of his life.

His last communication he controlled Alan himself, with no-one helping him out. He came along in fact to give guidance and advice to a person who had come for a private sitting. He came as someone giving help to someone else.

THE MERCENARY

The man was chained by his wrists to iron rings in the rough walls of the building. He had been fed just enough to keep him alive. His body bore a great many signs of torture - burns, slashes, grazes and bruises everywhere. He knew he had at least two of his ribs broken and his genitals were swollen and bloody from the heavy booted kicking he had to endure every morning and night.

His glazed eyes were closed to help him bear the pain of his body. There were no individual pains now - just one long blur of aching. He knew it was only a matter of time. He knew also that there was still the Big Man to come and have his kicks. His captors told him every day, as they brought him his food.

'Keep you alive for the Big Man, Boy!'

They were mostly drunk. They considered they deserved to be, having captured a mercenary - especially one as tough and important as this. None of their group had ever caught out one of these, almost legendary white fighters, and this was why the Big Man was coming. It was certainly an honour for them that he was coming.

At last he arrived. He WAS a big man in all senses of the word. Grotesquely huge, obese with over indulgence, his face bloated, cruel, and dissipated. He forced up the prisoner's head, and slapped him hard, opening up the taught skin across his cheekbones. The Big Man smiled watching his victim's blood trickling down the paths of dried blood and excrement smattered over the prisoner's face. He then brought up his huge boot to kick him over and over again in the groin.

But the prisoner had seen a spark of brilliant light near to where his head had fallen. He stared at it in wonder and it grew and grew in brilliance and size. In the light he could see a face forming - a face with eyes that smiled at him, that calmed him, that seemed to comfort and protect him. A hand was extended from that light towards him and the mercenary reached up and took the hand - totally oblivious of the pulping of his genitals into a mess of blood and raw flesh.

At once he merged into the light and was taken away from the turgid scene of the ugly, kicking man, and the limp mass that was once his body.

PART FOUR

This part of the book, gives the experiences of two people who developed cancer. As you have read up to now, everyone has a totally different experience of moving from the only world they know - this physical world - into the next world, the Spiritual world. I use this word 'Spiritual' to mean 'non-physical' and for no other meaning.

Because so many people have died, and do die from this disease, it is not possible to say that there is 'One' way of dying.

Everyone's pain threshold is so different, and also their attitude to pain varies so much, and there can be no single statement of how a person dying from cancer must be suffering. All experience differently.

We were carrying out some trance healing for a terminal cancer patient, who lived several thousand miles away from us. I was holding a personal possession of the patient, and I felt totally merged with that patient throughout the whole of the healing. It was not a pleasant experience, I can assure you - due, in my opinion, to the accumulation of drugs in that person's body. I can still remember the inability to get my mind clear. This feeling of absolute muzziness was intense, it took me over and it was impossible to escape it.

I have experienced quite a lot of pain in my life - and I know that pain can be handled. It does seem to help to be able to moan and groan a little! I must say that pain was far preferable to me than that state of complete haziness, where I had no idea of any quality of existence whatsoever.

I really believe that this human experience is not intended to bring to the body unbearable, excruciating pain. It would serve no purpose. Even the Mercenary, whose life was seemingly one of giving and receiving all manner of torture, had his pain diffused into an all over ache. For others in this book, unconsciousness took them away from pain.

So perhaps, if people try to handle their own pain a little, there would be no need to be given so many harmful drugs, and the last moments of their life could be experienced far differently.

BOB

I died on September 21st 1963. I was at the time ill -
suffering from cancer of the lung. I had not been ill for too
long, and I was lucky, I suppose, not to have spent a long time
in my bed. My family had to put up with the problem from a
different angle - and no doubt they were lucky too that it was
not prolonged.

To begin at the beginning - well as near the beginning
as we need for the purpose of this narrative, I was born in
Louisiana in the United States of America, in the year 1924. I
was the only son of a fairly prosperous farmer, and I became a
teacher at a local university - by local, I mean in the state of
Louisiana.

I had met and married my wife by the time I was twenty five and we had settled down to a busy life on the campus of
my college.

My wife was also a teacher but in the field of physical
training. She ran teams for inter-varsity ball games and sports
of all kinds. Hers was a far more physically demanding job
than was mine and, in many respects our lives became a little
separated.

When I was free, she was busy working. We had no
time it seemed for raising a family. I was quite keen on a largish family, but my wife didn't stand still long enough to pro-
duce even one child - I don't blame her of course for this - having children is a two-person happening.

So we went on as do most couples. My own interests
outside of teaching lay in the garden and growing things, and
also in nature and picking the wild harvests and turning them
into food and drink. It seems strange that we were perhaps the
wrong way round - certainly for the hopes I had of a family.
Had my wife been of my mind and I of hers, no doubt we
would have had a large, noisy, bickering family - just as I had
wished for. I, however would have been far too busy in my
games and competitions to be bothered with them and they
would have been brought up one-sided - so much for dreams!

142

As can be expected, my marriage began to fail. Our interests were too opposite, but it seemed that neither one of us wanted to make the break and set up home on our own somewhere. Also we were both stubborn about our jobs - neither one wanted to find someplace else. So we drifted along like so many people do.

We stayed together, argued almost whenever we came into contact with each other, and were much happier when we didn't. Eventually of course other people started to come into our lives. I met a few girls who were just as keen on picking berries as I and naturally we started making arrangements to meet and pick berries together.

Then we discussed recipes - often these girls were quite amused to find a guy who could understand their own ideas, and so my lovely days out in the countryside were even more pleasurable. Of course things soon became more involved and one thing led to another. On my own part they never led to the ultimate togetherness of a man and a woman.

Then my wife began bringing home men friends who were involved as she was, in the world of fitness. Her other life began when a guy called on the phone to ask if she were interested in setting up a series of ball games for television - one of our local networks.

I had originally taken the call and had to admit, that Jerry was a nice guy to talk to. He knew how to listen and also how to handle anyone's hang-ups - or hobbies. He was a kind of all-rounder. So he came into our mess of a marriage and immediately brought a new situation into being. From the first meeting with him, in our lounge, my wife was lost. Even I could see that.

She began spending time away, due to setting up out of town matches and interviewing players and sports people from out of our state. She soon was using the house more as a motel than a home, and it became obvious that I was going to have to make some kind of stand. I put this off and kept doing so.

We drifted along and the years passed. It seemed that Jerry also had some other kinds of commitments, that he had no wish to break up, and so my wife just kept on hanging in

143

there. I feel sure though, in my heart that she did not really want to commit herself any more than did Jerry, to a full-time marriage with anyone. They were each happy just drifting along, meeting up as much as possible with their work as stimulant to their meetings.

In time there were a few other 'Jerry's', and somehow, I could not bring myself to pack up, quit my job and leave her to it. It seemed to me that was her duty - not mine. After all I had not been the first to bring others into my life. In fact there were only a couple of women I had shown any kind of interest in, and neither of these were prepared to have an affair with a wife hanging about and appearing from time to time on a regular basis.

So, I developed a more 'alone' situation. The only time I conversed with people was during my lectures. Gradually even my pleasure in the countryside diminished as did my culinary interests and hobbies. Instead I developed a large drink habit. A solitary, large drink habit.

I had always been fond of music, and soon my life had a definite pattern to it - work for five days and the other two days were spent at home no matter what weather was happening outside. At home with my eternal long-playing records and my large, eternal Scotch and sodas. I exercised as little as possible - which meant a walk to the college, then at lunch break, to the dining hall, then back to my class, then home.

I forgot to mention my other really bad habit - I smoked constantly. It was known as chain-smoking. As soon as one cigarette butt was stabbed out, I lit up another cigarette. At night I did my schoolwork always with a couple of large Scotch's alongside an overflowing ash tray. Then I put on my music and cried into my glass till it was time to go to my solitary bed.

By the time I was thirty nine, I knew I had had it. I had developed a hacking cough which had put me off work, as I couldn't talk without coughing and I couldn't cough without a lot of blood - my blood, staining my handkerchiefs.

As I did my own laundry, and as my wife had moved long ago into another bedroom, she was not really aware of how bad my problem was. I had been off work for three weeks. I had seen a doctor and he had sent me to get my chest X-rayed. The results had come out and I was due to go into the hospital for surgery.

My wife did not know of this as she was out of the state working full-time for a TV Sports channel. Why she did not pack up her bags when she landed this job, and leave me to it, I could not imagine. She got home one weekend in three, and sometimes she would put in mid week appearances for a couple of days, during which she would just lie around on the verandah soaking up the sun, or spend time in the sauna and the gymnasium she had set up in the spare room.

So off I went to the hospital, leaving her a note saying where I was, but not the true reason why. I knew even before I was wheeled along that long corridor, that I would not survive the surgery. I had known this for a few weeks before I had even had the X-rays. In my lucid moments first thing in the morning, after my coughing sessions to remove as much as I could of the blood and fluids from my battered lungs, I had thought about what I should do regarding putting things in order.

Although I had seen little of my parents since my marriage went wrong, I wrote and told them I was ill and would be going into hospital for surgery, but I did not want them rushing over. I would write again as soon as I was feeling better. My parents were not young - they had me late on in their lives, and they were not used to rushing about the state. Any visiting had to be done by me since I married. I told them not to worry.

Then I wrote a long letter to my wife in which I tried to tell her of my feelings and reasons for drinking etcetera. I didn't blame her in any way. It was a difficult letter to write and it took me three attempts until I was satisfied with it.

Then after such heroic efforts - I needed a drink and some lovely soothing music because wasn't I just the world's most 'hard done to' person? You bet your life I was!

I didn't worry about bills and suchlike as we had never been financially unstable and there was ample in deposit accounts to pay what was due. Somehow I felt I had to put all to rights and that's just what I had done.

The very last thing I can remember is a pair of lovely, dark brown - almost black eyes looking down into mine above a white cotton mask, and a soft voice asking me to count to ten, as she injected the vein in my arm.

The next thing I can remember is my name being called over and over again by my wife. She was driving along the highway in her English sports car - and somehow, I was there with her. I was sitting in the passenger seat aware of all that was going on. We were speeding along and I soon recognised we were going in the direction of the hospital. I tried to answer her calling my name but she took no notice at all - just kept on saying it over and over again.

She was driving fast as usual, and I was a bit worried we might have an accident. I hung on to the strap, or at least I tried to but that durned strap kept eluding my hand! For some reason I could not guess, I was not able to take a hold of it.

At last we turned into the hospital grounds and my wife parked the car and, without even looking at me, she got out and rushed off to the operating building. Somehow I was with her all of the way. I cannot remember running; getting out of the car; closing the door or any of these things. I just know that I was as close as it was possible to be, to my wife as she hurried along.

Soon we were in the small room alongside of the theatre, and there the surgeon and his nurse were telling my wife gently that I had died during the operation. It was news to me! I felt so alive - my wife had at last stopped repeating my name, and I saw she was really upset - really sorry that I had died. I also saw - just as if she was telling it to me herself - that she was feeling sorry for ME - not herself!

She was thinking back over our life together and feeling so sad for me. She wished she could have been different, she seemed to say, but she was as she was. I felt that at least she was honest and I felt a warm glow as I realised this. At that moment it seemed that I knew my wife better than I had ever known her. I understood her feelings. Then everything went black - I passed out.

When I came round again, I could hear many people

calling my name - it went on and on. My parents; my wife; my friends - or should I say acquaintances; my working colleagues; my neighbours; some of my students. I put my hands over my ears because I could not stand the noise of it all. My head started to ache and I wanted a drink.

I was thinking how could I slope off and put on some music and relax with my cigarettes and my glasses of Scotch? Somehow though, I had to stay with it and put up with all of this noise of my name. I began to hate my name and I felt the old familiar panic coming on - just as when, in my usual routine, I had drunk that one over the top, and smoked that last cigarette, and my head reeled. I gave in to the dizziness and lost consciousness.

When I came to, this time, all was blissfully quiet. I reached into my pocket for my cigarettes, but there were none there. The longing was just beginning in me for nicotine, when a voice alongside of me said 'Hi, I'm Angelo!'

Standing beside me was a guy in jeans and a bright T-shirt, and shiny black boots with heels. He was a nice-looking, fair haired fellow, with a very friendly grin. He looked a bit different and I wondered why until I realised that his hair was a bit long - a hippy-type long. He was from the South, too, and was studying me as much as I was studying him.

'D'ya want to come for a walk - see somethin' of the place?' Angelo asked, smiling.

'Why not?' I answered.

We walked round for maybe an hour - he showed me all manner of places - mainly countryside and farms and small holdings. Then we went along to some place where people - men and women were harvesting fruits and berries. Everyone was extremely happy and singing and laughing. There was something a bit foreign about them and they were quite poorly dressed compared to our standards.

I asked Angelo where we were and he said Eastern Europe somewhere. These were peasants, it seemed, and they were getting in the harvest - but not for themselves. All farms belonged to the State, and these people were very poorly paid indeed. They were not far away from starvation in comparison

147

to what I was used to. After watching for a while, I said to Angelo 'So, why are we watching these poor people?'

'Interesting,' he said.

'Yeh, I'm sure it is, but there has to be a reason,' I replied.

'It just makes a picture of how you can be happy with very little,' Angelo remarked, and, all of a sudden, we were no longer there in that pleasant countryside.

I think I felt rather than saw the next situation, first. It was a scene of someone's privacy, and my feelings told me I should not like what was to come, or indeed what was going on.

The woman was a good-looker in all aspects. She was totally naked as was the much older guy with her. It was a very luxurious pad - could have been in any country, I suppose - any country, any town - but only in a very wealthy district. Opulence was everywhere, in the furnishings and the decor and the lighting, and the video equipment that was filming all that was going on.

I will not describe the action because it was pathetic in truth. My overall feeling was of the state of mind of these two people - because it sure was a joint effort. It was a pure case of perversion, materially, these two people had all there was to have and now needed something else to stimulate their appetites.

The filming showed also that there were a great many like-minded people who would take part in this kind of act - either as voyeurs or as imitators.

I closed my eyes to this scene and almost as soon as I did so, Angelo and I were out in a pleasant green valley, sitting alongside a gurgling stream. A gentle breeze blew over me and, I felt, seemed to be taking away the scene so recently etched on to my senses. It took away the feelings of what I saw, but of course my thoughts were still with it. I felt quiet and did not want to talk.

Angelo seemed to understand, and he was silently watching the antics of a small bird on a branch of a nearby tree. As I watched him watching, my thoughts gradually became

148

immersed, because the little bird, I could swear was aware of our gaze, and seemed to be putting on a little show, just for us. It was hopping and fluttering over and under the branch, catching hold first with one claw then with the other - at times seeming almost to fall and then recovering its balance again.

I laughed at one point and Angelo said 'Interesting how the mind can be handled, aint it?'

'Yeh,' I replied, understanding immediately exactly what he was getting at.

'But how do we move around as we have done?'

'Using the mind,' he said.

I thought about this for a while but could not grasp it at all.

'Anything you especially want to do or see?' Angelo asked.

'No, I feel I want a space to sort things out,' I replied and as I looked at him, he disappeared. I think he said 'OK, see ya' but I was not sure because he just went. He didn't stand up and walk away - he just was not there anymore.I stretched full length on the grass, face down, my head on my arms and fell asleep.

I awoke to the sounds of laughter - children's laughter. I got up and found I was in a totally different place - it seemed like a children's yard at school. There were all manner of swings and frames of intricate design for climbing. There was gymnastic equipment, there were bridges over a small stream edged with trees. There were kids riding bikes of a very simple basic design, but with no brakes, I noticed.

I watched them for a while wondering how they would manage when they came to an obstacle. One girl of about six was riding along towards the stream, and, as she approached it, the bike just stopped it seemed at a command from her of 'Stop!' She seemed delighted at this and laughed loudly each time her bike obeyed her command.

There were other games going on and little adventures. The atmosphere was one of true happiness as only a child can experience. As I watched a young woman came up to me smiling.

149

'Hello' she greeted me, 'I'm Pat. I work here, can I show you round?'

'Yeah, I would be happy,' I said, taking in her easy grey eyes and fresh appearance. She was as tall as I and slim. I was a little taken aback at her gown, which seemed a bit dressy for working in a kid's play yard.

'I wear it because it is so easy to wear,' she explained to my acute embarrassment. Then she laughed. 'You can't hide your thoughts here' she said.I reddened and felt the warmth of my gaucheness, but she was still smiling and looked away towards the schoolhouse.

'Come and look over our school, I am sure you will like it.'

We walked along together and I found to my surprise, that without my asking or her telling, I was beginning to know a great deal about Pat. She was English and had been here quite a few years. She loved kids and whenever she could get the chance, came over here to the school to work. When she was not here she worked in several places doing various things all of which were her hobbies and abilities.

One of her greatest loves was designing pieces of equipment for educational and therapeutical exercises. She used to be a teacher way back, and had always felt frustrated for those kids with disabilities. She used to feel strongly that somehow they could be encouraged, with good equipment, to improve their abilities in many ways.

In her life however, there had not been the resources to develop such equipment, and she had not been extrovert enough to push for what she felt was needed, with those who had the money and power. Here it was different, and she was using her newly found strength to pass some of her ideas to people still living on earth. So life was good for her.

I was astounded to realise just how much I was able to know about her - and not a little embarrassed.

'Don't worry' she said looking at me, 'you'll get used to it.'

'I don't know about that,' I replied. 'Seems to me a person should be a little more private.'

'You are if you want to be, or if you are on a different wavelength. As you and I are quite compatible - of a similar mind in lots of ways, then it is like a natural friendship, without the need for time to get to know one another. It's instant knowledge and instant friendship, but of course you cannot know anything I would not want you to know about me - and vice versa. I am aware of yourself from the point of view of your likes, dislikes, abilities and disabilities. However, I do not judge you in any way, just as you do not judge me. We are just aware of each other's being, I suppose you could say.'

This was rather a lot for me to understand at that moment, so I accepted it and spent a happy time in her company, as she showed me around the fascinating building used to teach the kids who died early on in their lives on the earth. It seemed like a kind of consolation for the loss they had sustained, I thought at first, but then I realised that they had in reality not lost anything in dying from a harsh world of physical deprivation, as well as abuse and the lack of love, which is the lot of so many.

Everywhere here, the people appeared to have a lot of love and time to give the kids.

After our pleasant time together, Pat excused herself as she had an appointment, and left me where she had picked me up - in the school yard, alongside the stream, and laughing with the little girl who had pedalled towards me at full speed on her bike, only to stop a few feet in front of me, because her mind had commanded the bike to do so.

My experiences in this new world were like that - one minute laughing and basking in the warmth of friendship and companionship, another minute finding joy in nature or the innocent fun of children, and yet another minute being made fully aware of the lengths to which man will go to squeeze some kind of enjoyment from the very dregs of behaviour. Of course 'minutes' do not really come into it, but it is the easiest way to describe things to you. Sometimes the experiences seemed to last an awful long time, and sometimes they were all too brief.

Although I had not really considered deeply, the possibility of a life after death, I had not decided in my mind it was not possible. I just really had not investigated the matter. My mind had gone along different paths of interest.

It was not difficult though, for me to realise what had happened because my death was not dramatic in any way - there was no dividing line between my life and my death. There were no 'angels' or 'harps' or 'God' to be aware of.

There was no time of great distress that I remember - perhaps a little frustration, at knowing things which I could do nothing about, where the physical world was concerned.

I suppose I could describe my death as an interesting experience - perhaps the most interesting experience I had ever had in my life!

NELLIE

It was ten o'clock in the morning. I had looked at my watch four times in the last hour. Surely the doctor must come soon - Alf had rung for him. All I could do was wait and try not to think or wonder about the problem. Try not to think about the blood which even now was soaking into the pads that Alf had placed under me.

It was a strange situation to be in. I had gone through a lot of pain having the children - four I'd had and each one, except the second, June, had been difficult, with a lot of blood lost. Then I'd had blood transfusions and plenty of iron to strengthen my blood, the doctor said.

I'd always tried to eat the right things because my mother used to insist that I ate plenty of liver and spinach - of all things! I don't know if Popeye had anything to do with that, but my mother always swore by spinach. The problem was it became hard to get in later years. We had always known a man with an allotment, who grew spinach - he probably went to the same school as my mother! Anyway, he passed on, and the shops didn't have the same belief in spinach as those two!

I had continued in my life to try to keep my blood

healthy with the right food and plenty of fresh greens. Now here it was leaving my body again.

I wasn't feeling bitter or anything - just tired. The pains were duller now, I suppose because I had taken painkillers the doctor had left a few days ago. He had wanted me to go into the hospital, but me and Alf decided I was better here at home. We both knew I hadn't too long to go. I had got to a good age, I suppose, seventy six.

I had sorted out a few things and made a will. Not that I had much to leave, but my children would like to know I thought about them - even though they lived so far away now. I left personal things that I thought they would like - much better than them coming along and scrambling about amongst it all. Of course it was only my own things I had left them. Alf was still a very healthy man, and no doubt would go on much longer than me.

We had talked a bit last night - before this latest rush of blood started. He wondered if I was frightened of dying. It was funny to see him trying to ask me - even after all of these years together. We didn't really know each other in a deep sense. Oh, we knew how each would react to things, and we knew what the other liked in the world and disliked in the world. We never really ever got down to deeper things though, in fact we rarely spoke our true minds on things that were happening in our life.

It was always as if one wanted to please the other - even if it came to being untruthful. When Alf was in a corner he would always go quiet and I knew not to push him. He used to have quite a temper when he was a bit younger, and because I always wanted a quiet life, with no fuss or arguments, I backed off and changed the subject. I always let him have his own way really I suppose. Because of his temper.

I had my pride of course but it never seemed so important that I should stand up to him or anyone, come to think of it. I always used to think, 'They'll soon find out who's right.' So I always left it. My eldest daughter, Gwen, always used to say 'Mother's closed her mouth with that little look of hers!' She was right - I did just that. It meant 'I'm saying no more on the subject.'

153

People have always thought I was strong I suppose because I always have just got on with things. They could never see how I really felt though. No-one could - only me. It was a kind of crying, I suppose - inside. My pride never let me cry outside, or only rarely. It was how I was brought up, not to show your feelings.

It tired me though, not showing my feelings and keeping everything deep inside. It was the same when the children got married or left home. I mustn't show my feelings, but oh, it was hard to let them go. I had a special relationship with them, I like to think. They were all different and I liked to treat them different. Of course I never told them how I felt about them - ever! Kept it all inside like everything else.

Sometimes now I wonder about that - whether I was right, because oh, it did hurt inside as each of them left home. Just like it did the other night before the doctor came, and the nights before that, when I said nothing to Alf. I suppose I had been in pain for a couple of months before I let it out.

I didn't want to be a problem to Alf and I didn't want to become dependent on him or go into the hospital. Amazing what a human being can suffer when they have a mind!

It's funny really, but this flowing of my blood isn't unpleasant. I know it is happening and the warmth is somehow comforting.

I have had some strange dreams just lately - and not always when asleep. Mostly they concern people who have gone before. Sometimes I have long talks with them - old friends and relations. All nice and natural. I suppose it is something to do with getting old. You tend to look back and not forward. There is not a great deal to look forward to when you get older. You start to live for the day and your little plans around the house, and the odd days out. No doubt this is the reason old people look back. It is amazing just how vivid those thoughts are though.

I'm not keen on the mess poor Alf has to sort out. It's not right for a man to have to do it, but he says it doesn't bother him, and he is glad to do something for me. I suppose it is his conscience because he still gets down to the pub for his pint

154

and I am stuck here in bed.

I just went a bit funny then - a bit dizzy and the room spun. Good job I am in bed. It must be the weakness of losing so much blood. I feel all right now though - it was just for a few seconds.

No, I don't worry about dying because I think I have done my best. My mother said 'Always do your best, you can't do any more.' She was right. I do worry a bit though about not saying what I thought about things, but then there were always circumstances.

Oh there's the door - it's the doctor. That's strange he's taking my pulse and feeling my heart.

'That's it' he's told Alf. 'It's over, I'm afraid.'

Well this is strange, I must say. I seem to be following Alf and the doctor downstairs. I feel all right. I am solid enough, so I can't be a ghost of myself. How strange this all is. I am walking as if I were really fit - I feel fit. I feel very light and floaty and here comes Vi, my old school friend, who used to live next door. Even when I married she somehow managed to finish up living next door! Dear Vi! She's holding her arms out to me and I can feel her love all round me - what a strange sensation, so warm and happy. Should I feel so happy, when the doctor has just said 'It's over'?

'It IS over dear!' Vi said. 'Come along with me and we'll have a lovely rest together.'

PART FIVE

This part of the book has just one person's experiences. It tells of how she felt she had reached her limit, in dealing with her life. It also tells of how much more there was for her to understand about herself, and the choices she made.

There was very strong contact when this lady gave me her experiences. I feel that she, above all the rest, is anxious that her story be told, and that we all realise that there is so much more to situations than we realise.

INGRID

I was a teacher in an infant's school. I loved my work because I loved children. I had never married, and at the age of forty three, I certainly did not expect to ever change that situation.

Life, however, can have some very unexpected happenings - one day there you are, a spinster teacher, and then all of a sudden, someone comes into your life and everything changes.

I met Ted at a concert. I was very fond of music - especially amateur productions, and I had promised a friend I would go to the Gilbert and Sullivan performance they were putting on.

It was a lovely performance and we all thoroughly enjoyed it. Afterwards, my friend, flush from her efforts, met me as arranged in the small bar upstairs and we sat at a table having a drink and talking about the evening. A man brushed past our table and inadvertently caught my glass with his coat. The result was a bright pool of sherry all over the table and this man apologised and tried to mop up the mess with his handkerchief.

Then surprisingly enough, in a half hour, there this man was, seated at our table, having brought us fresh drinks. He had introduced himself as the music critic for the local paper, and asked our permission to join us.

That was the beginning of the total over-turning of my ordered life. After a whirlwind courtship, if I may use such an old-fashioned word (though it was not old-fashioned at the time), I became Mrs. Edward Winston. That was when all my troubles began.

Ted was a Jekyll and Hyde character. He told the most involved lies and I feel he used to believe in it all himself. He was exceedingly cruel underneath a most courteous exterior. Had I told any of my dearest friends of very long standing, I am afraid they would never have believed me.

When my health finally broke down, not so long after our marriage, everyone put it down to my age and the enormous change marriage had brought. Ted was always so extremely polite and considerate to everyone, and of course long friendship does breed a degree of familiarity, so, for some reason, I became, in their eyes, a little eccentric.

From the beginning, Ted insisted that I leave my post and become a housewife. He was determined to support me on his own earnings. The music critic job did not exist, and it may seem hard for you to believe, but I had no idea where Ted got his money. He used to go out each morning around eight o'clock and return each evening about six o'clock, for five days of the week.

One day I decided to follow him, so curious was I. Unfortunately, he caught a bus just as I emerged from the house, and, although I saw the back of it going up the road, it was a road which many buses used, and I was unable to know which one it had been. Our city was rather a large place, and it was quite simple for a person to just disappear from sight by hopping on to a bus or just turning a corner. Of course I tried several times to find out where he went, but never once did I succeed. In the end I gave it up as a bad job.

Life became quite unpleasant when Ted started talking about our having a lodger, to help with expenses. He put a card it seems, in a newsagent's shop, and not long afterwards a young girl came knocking on our door.

She told a very sad story and I decided to tell Ted about

her when he got home and then, when she called back the next day, I would be able to let her know.

He was agreeable - in fact he did not show too much interest, even though it had been his idea. The house, my own family house, where I had grown up, was quite large and we could well afford to let a couple of large attic rooms off.

The girl moved in. Moira was her name, She was Irish and was working as a domestic for an agency. Because of this her hours were never quite regular, she came and went at all hours.

Then one day things really developed in an unpleasant way. Ted had gone off to his mysterious 'work', and I was supposed to be going to the other side of town to visit an old friend. However, in the post that very morning, I received a note from her putting me off until the next day, due to some unforeseen circumstance. So I decided to get out into the garden and clear up a patch of bedding plants right at the back of the garden, behind our old greenhouse.

I suppose I spent a good two hours there, weeding and generally tidying it up. You can imagine my amazement, when, on coming out from behind the greenhouse, I got a very good view, through the attic window, of Ted and our lodger, totally in the nude, locked in a close embrace. At that moment, as I stared my mouth wide open in amazement, Ted looked down and saw me.

Life became very strange from then on. Nothing was said about the situation - it was as if it had never happened. Ted did not come down when I went back into the house, and I felt I just could not go up there and confront them. It was as if I was living some kind of fantasy life as those two acted as if nothing had ever happened and things were just as normal.

This time I could not confide in anyone. They would not believe me. Several times I started to tell my really close friend Grace, but the words stuck in my throat. I got depressed, especially as Ted and the girl seemed to go out of their way now to touch as they passed, or look deeply into each other's eyes, oblivious of my being there. I started to think he had planned it all right from suggesting we advertise for a lodger.

Every day strange happenings occurred in the house - nothing was ever in its right place, as if I had left them around and not put them back. We had arguments over this - me insisting I had and Ted insisting that I was losing my memory and hadn't. Broken dishes were found in cupboards - certainly not put there by me.

I realised of course that Ted was pushing me to my limit. I lost weight and began to look old before my time. My hands got shaky because my nerves were getting frayed. I spilt things and of course dropped things and Ted played on all of this, to send me further into my nervous breakdown.

Finally I went out one night and jumped off a bridge into the river.

The strangest thing was that I wanted to end it all. I had wanted to die but although I was aware of a bursting in my lungs as the oxygen was replaced by water, I did not really lose consciousness. I was aware of watching my body as it went down deeper and deeper. I would have expected the water to be dark, but I could still see as if I was projecting a light myself.

Then I was no longer interested in my body and the river, because I felt a presence alongside of me. It was a warm enveloping presence that reminded me of when I was small and had fallen and was comforted by my mother's arms around me. The presence seemed to tell me everything was all right. I must admit that I did not totally feel all right - my nervous state was too heightened for that, but I certainly did not feel quite as alone as I had felt in my unpleasant life.

I spent a long time after that in some kind of cocoon. Sometimes there was silence around me and sometimes I could hear faint music. People did not exist as far as I was concerned - even the presence that had helped me into this new state of being, did not come near me. I knew somehow, that my allowing the mental suffering to go on for so long - my acceptance of the situation, had worn my very being, my spirit, to a very low ebb.

I was not in a fit state to join my life as it should have been. I had developed in myself a deep mistrust, even hatred for the human being, because I had found no-one to help or

159

succour me. So I was alone until somehow I could develop a little strength. From time to time I became aware of a kind of motion and warmth, as if I were being rocked in the sunshine somewhere. In time I came to look forward to these experiences and I think I developed a little strength from them. It took a very long time indeed before I was finally able to bear thoughts and ideas concerning my life, and when these thoughts came, I was flabbergasted.

It was as if I had gone to the pictures. There was a large screen and a film showing of an army of some kind. The soldiers were not really in uniform as such, but they all wore protective wooden and metal shields about them. They were occupied in marching towards a small village or encampment - it was a little too dark for me to be sure.

They moved stealthily and when they attacked, they certainly had the element of surprise on their side. The scenes that opened out were most unpleasant - raping, looting, pillaging, torturing, killing. Men, women and children too, underwent the most horrific experiences at the hands of these men. I did not really want to look, but somehow I felt compelled. I was drawn to one fellow who was especially ferocious towards children, and I could hardly bear to see his progress. Eventually all was quiet. The lucky ones had escaped, the rest were dead and dying. The man I was drawn to had in tow a young boy, a servant of some sorts it seemed.

The boy rushed to carry out orders flung at him and he never appeared to get things right for his master, because he was kicked, pushed and assaulted in all manner of horrible ways. The army used the facilities of this settlement until the morning came and they then started a ferocious fire and left in a straggling column.

I noticed the servant boy was tied to his master by a longish rope and was still receiving harsh treatment at the man's hands. The scene then faded away.

By then I knew without the shadow of a doubt that I had been that man. Ted had been the servant boy.

It took me a very long time looking into myself to know what it was that made up my character. I eventually began to recognise certain attitudes of mind that I had held during my unmarried years. Where children were concerned, I know I never could do enough for them at school. It did not make me a good teacher though - certainly not a wise one. I was not doing what I did for the right reasons of course - it was for myself, to satisfy some guilt feelings I had within me.

I realised in time just how selfish I was. No wonder I had never been popular with boys when I was young and young men when I was older! I had put it down to being an only one and not being able to mix - but it was something else, deeper than that.

I was really a taker. I did not give of myself in friend-ships. I used people for my own ends. Also I was a coward. When it came to a showdown or a challenge, I had always taken cover in a crowd. I always needed support, for I had no stamina on my own. No wonder I had never left my parent's house. I had never nursed them because I worked, so we hired nurses to do that when necessary. My parents both died in hos-pitals, so I did not even give to them at the end of their lives.

Now, at this moment, I am beginning my climb back to life. This story is my first offering. I offer it in the hope that someone, may benefit from my mistakes. If I can just make you stop and think about your reasons for what you do.

If you will realise that things and people are not what they seem, and that when tragedy happens - be sure to know that someone, somewhere is probably learning the biggest les-son about themselves that they could ever learn.

PART SIX

This section contains just two stories. They are as different as can be, and deal with experiences of death during war.

I never cease to be amazed at the ways in which children are helped into their life after death. There is, of course a special problem here, for generally their parents are still living and there is no-one to greet them that they know.

In Angela's case, it was slightly different from this view, and it seemed as though it was she who helped her mother.

ANGELA

There was an air raid expected in a few hours time. As a child of seven this did not mean a lot to me. All I knew was that my mother would pack something to eat and drink in a carrier bag, plus something to read and a torch in case we needed it, and we would all go down to the underground. Once there we would meet up with friends who had the same routine.

We used to all sit down - it was difficult for us children to have to sit down meekly with the adults. We were not allowed to run about as we should have liked. Of course at the beginning, when we would first get down there, a few would start playing and running about, but they would soon be jumped on by the wardens, if not their mothers or aunties or grandads.

Then for the next few hours we would occupy ourselves in games of 'I Spy' or, if it was darker due to electricity failures, we would play 'Shadows', making animal shapes with our hands held up twisted in odd ways.

There were times when it was 'total blackout' - when there were no torches to be lit because our area was a possible target. That was very eerie and I was not at all keen on those times. You just had to sit there - or sleep if you could. I was never tired in the daytime though and it was an awful experience for me. I did use to get the giggles sometimes, when a friend would set me off and then I wouldn't be able to stop and I would get a slap from my mother, which often did the trick!

When it was all black and if any of my usual friends were not near us, I used to sit there in the darkness, listening to all of the noises around me - they weren't at all pleasant, I might add! Then I would shut my eyes and try to imagine silence. It was sometimes very funny because as soon as I shut my eyes, I would see a really bright light! Then I would quickly open them again thinking someone had got the electricity working again, and I would be able to read!

However, it would still be dark in the tunnel, the platforms filled with people's shapes just visible in the gloom. People whispering or talking in their normal voices and some talking quite loudly as some do in the darkness - as if the loss of seeing also meant the loss of hearing!

This particular day, when we had no lights, none of my friends were around me, so I closed my eyes and waited to see if the light would come. It did, and not only the light but colours. What colours! It was much better than seeing the rainbow - everywhere was a mass of moving, changing colours, like a kaleidoscope being constantly turned and shaken.

I was fascinated by it all and very engrossed. Then somehow these colours began to take the shape of things - masses of greens began to look a bit like trees and lawns of grass, like playing fields, but stretching far into the distance. Every now and then my mother or someone would talk to me and disturb what I was seeing. When this happened it often took a long time for me to get the pictures back again. I just kept getting the colours.

However I was so keen on seeing the trees and things, and hoped I might get something else, that I asked my Mum not to prod me with her elbow. I said I didn't want anything to eat or drink, but just wanted to be allowed to watch the colours. I explained what I was seeing but my mum wasn't too interested because she wasn't able to see anything but darkness when she closed her eyes.

So I had a very long session of seeing the colours and

shapes. I was hoping that once the trees and grass were in place for a time without my having to open my eyes and lose them, I might just get to see some fairies. I didn't tell Mum this because I feared it might not happen if she knew.

I had a lovely picture of a group of trees, not a wood exactly, but several trees with lovely green leaves shimmering away and tufts of grasses, some darker than others, some shorter than others, when suddenly, I seemed to be a part of the scene. It was as if I had jumped into the picture and was standing in the little clearing of trees and grass. I couldn't see myself of course, I just knew I was there. I even stretched out my hand to touch the trunk of a lovely tree near me. It was a lovely experience, my hand seemed to tingle as it contacted the tree trunk. The trunk felt hard but not hard! I know it sounds silly but that was how it felt.

The most exciting thing though was that my hand looked different! It seemed to be surrounded by a lovely bright light all around it and from my fingers I saw a stream of pretty soft yellow light. Odd, I thought, so I held up my hand and looked at it. From each finger light streamed upwards - made up of little tiny flecks of light, like the beam you see at the cinema, which went down to the screen. All of the bits of light were dancing about - not still. It was really lovely.

I looked down for some reason, to look at my feet. What a surprise! I didn't have my red shoes on, with the bows, I had instead some kind of gold slippers! I was amazed because I wondered if I had changed into a fairy. I remembered at one of our school fancy dress competitions, a girl I knew, whose family had the corner shop, came as a Christmas fairy and she had on some very lovely slippers her uncle had brought from China or somewhere. He was in the Merchant Navy and went everywhere. He always brought her lovely glittering things, and I wished my dad would go to sea and bring me lovely things. Anyway her slippers had jewels stuck on to them and had curled up toes as well with a jewel hanging from the point of the curl.

So then I looked down at my dress and again I was startled, because it wasn't my usual short dress, but a long one that stopped quite a bit below my knees. It didn't go down to my feet though. It was this dress that convinced me that I must have changed into a fairy, because it was made of the loveliest material, much better than Jenny's fairy dress. It was whitish, but in the white were all other colours, red and blue and green little flecks, all sparkling as if they were moving about like the bits in my kaleidoscope.

I was a bit overcome. I didn't know quite what to do, and just then a lady appeared from amongst the trees. She was really a lovely lady. She wore a long dress down to her feet. It was a lovely blue with bits of gold here and there, round the hem and sleeves and neck. This lady had long, dark hair, and I wondered if she was a film star because she really was lovely.

Anyway she smiled at me and said 'Hello Angela.'

I wondered how she knew my name and she said straightaway that she had come to meet me, knowing I would be coming along here to this little wood to see if there were any fairies about.

Although I wondered how she knew all this, I decided to hold her hand as she suggested and walk along a bit to where she thought we might find fairies.

Well we went along just a short way and then she stopped and sat down on a tree trunk and motioned me to do the same. She didn't speak but I knew she wanted me to be quiet. So as quietly as I could, I sat down and hardly dared breathe in case it made a noise. In front of us there was a patch of funny light. This light was different from the light around and it seemed to hang over a little bit of short grass that had grass a bit longer all round it, making a circle.

I realised it was a 'fairy ring'. I felt excited as I knew we were going to see fairies. Oh, how I would tell them all at school! I was quite fidgety but the lady put her hand on my arm and gently squeezed it to tell me to stay quiet in my thoughts. She didn't speak of course, but somehow I knew what she meant. I suppose fairies are disturbed if you get too excited and I didn't want them not to come.

Well, we didn't have to wait long. This little cloud of shimmering mist started to come down on the grass. When it was just settled it cleared and there were about twenty fairies - very, very tiny but very clear to my eyes. They were beautiful - all shimmering gold and white and always moving. None of them stayed still at all. They danced or ran or walked. Some leapt into the air and did somersaults. It was a lovely sight because the fairies were all dressed in different colours - all shimmering and so pretty.

Just as I was beginning to look at each fairy, trying to separate one from another, I felt a big squeeze and had to open my eyes. It was my mother, telling me it was time to go home - 'All Clear'.

Well, as you can imagine I was not too happy about this. There was nothing I could do however except help gather our things together and go home. I must say I was looking forward to the next air raid warning to come along. We had just got in the house and I was helping my mother unpack the food bag. There was a droning noise over the house and the next thing I knew, my mother had grabbed me and rushed us into the cupboard under the stairs. She was too late though - there was an enormous crash and the ceiling fell on top of us - the chimney coming with it.

My mother and I didn't know the chimney had come down - in fact I don't know what my mother knew, but I felt a big crack on my head and I knew nothing more.

It happened so quickly, one minute I was being pulled into the cupboard, and the next this sudden pain on my head - then nothing!

I must have gone to sleep in the hospital or something, because I remember waking up in bed in a hospital. I had a nurse looking after me, and as I opened my eyes she was there. I got such a shock on seeing her because I recognised her as the lady in the wood who took me to see the fairies.

She wasn't wearing the same long dress, but had on a white overall, like they have at the hospital, when you go to get your arm or leg put into plaster. I was quite pleased to see her and wanted to get up so that we could go and find the fairies again. However she told me I had to wait for a while, just a few minutes while she gave me some treatment to make me feel better.

166

I was a bit surprised at this because I felt very well. The only problem was that I was a bit confused, because I felt sure my mother had made me open my eyes just at the time I was looking at the fairies.

The lady smiled as I frowned trying to sort out my thoughts. She told me not to try but just close my eyes again for a few moments and she would be able to make me feel better. So I did as she asked and no sooner had I closed my eyes than a lovely warm, tingling feeling went all over me. I really felt nice, so I opened my eyes again. This time there was no hospital or bed. I was back in the wood with the lady in her long blue dress and we were sitting just where we were before. looking at the fairies dancing. I was really happy to see them and started to look hard again at each tiny form.

I don't know just how long I sat there entranced. I know it was quite as long as I had wished, and then the tiny figures all merged into one again and became this glimmering mist which hung over the grass ring. Then it lifted above the ground and gradually disappeared.

The lovely lady stood up and held out her hand. She didn't speak to me but somehow I knew we had somewhere else to go. I closed my eyes, for I felt she wanted me to.

When I opened them again, I was in a different place altogether. It was some kind of big park and there were people all around in little groups, talking together. Then I saw one or two girls I knew from my school and I rushed over to speak to them and to tell them about the fairies. When I looked round my friend had gone, but I didn't feel sad because I knew she would come back.

My friends had found some lovely swings, they said and did I want to go and play there. So off we went.

We played for a long time, with no-one bothering us. It was really good and I was enjoying myself. We found a lovely pool and, in a little hut near the pool, were lots of swimming costumes hanging on pegs. It was very strange because three of them had our names embroidered on them, so, because it was such a lovely day, we decided to get them on and play in the pool.

It was really marvellous - much better than the baths near our house. No-one splashed us and we were able to practise our swimming strokes and float very easily. When we had tired of the pool, we wondered if there were any towels to get dried with and when we went into the hut, found none...but we were dry! It was like magic.

Well we three found all kinds of things of interest around us. We climbed trees, walked through woods, looked at lovely beds of flowers, rowed ourselves in a nice boat we found tied up on a little river. There were lots of people around all of the time, but no-one told us off for borrowing the boat. We tied it up as we had found it and went off on our next little adventure.

There was a wonderful slide, right down the side of a hill, so it went on and on, going round the sides just like a helter skelter. We sat on little cushions and didn't go too fast. We were able to talk together as we watched the things about us coming and going from view.

Somehow it didn't seem to get dark. It certainly seemed a little darker - like at tea-time, when you knew you were going to be called in, just in the middle of a good game. But no-one called us in and so we went on coming across all kinds of new things to do and look at and ride in. It was the most marvellous place we had ever seen.

Then all of a sudden I saw my lady friend coming across the grass towards us. She was smiling at us and she held out her hands. We all managed to hold a bit of her hands and she laughingly asked us if we had enjoyed ourselves. Had we!

Well it was now time for us to help her in a job that was a bit difficult. She found a nice hump of grass and sat at the top of it and we three sat around her, just below her. First she had to tell us something we might not like. She asked us if we remembered the bombing and the underground. We did but it seemed so long ago. It was a long time ago she agreed but did we remember leaving the underground and going home?

It was then I got a picture in my mind - very clearly of my mother pulling me towards the cupboard under the stairs and then the ceiling fell in and I felt that big pain on my head.

At that moment everything wobbled a bit and the lady put her hand gently on my head. The wobbling stopped and I was all right again. The lady put her hand on the other two, so I knew they must have felt a bit wobbly as well.

Then she told us what had happened to each of us. Our chimney had fallen in on to my mother and I, a factory wall had toppled on to one of the others and the third girl's house had been hit by a bomb. We all felt a bit unhappy at this news. The lady was telling us that we had died.

I asked about our mothers and the lady smiled and told us we were going to see our mothers to comfort them and to show them that we were all right. It was important though that we realised that our life we had before was now over. There would be no more bombs or underground or gas masks. She asked if we had enjoyed ourselves since we had come together, and of course we had. This would be our new world, she had told us, and there were lots more interesting things to do and see - and also people we could help as well.

Then she asked us to join hands with her and each other and we formed a little ring. Then we had to close our eyes and the next thing I knew, was that we were back at that nice place where we had all met. We were walking along a pathway leading up to a big house with steps at the front. It was like those big hotels at the seaside.

When we went into the hallway, I saw my Mum sitting on her own at a little table. I rushed up to her and when she saw me she started crying and sobbing as she put her arms around me. I tried to comfort her and I touched her face and smiled at her. I told her I was all right and happy and asked her to come for a walk and I would try to show her the fairies.

I decided to try what the lady had done with me. I held my mum's hand and we went down the steps into the garden. I told my mum to close her eyes and I closed mine and wished us to be where the fairies were.

It worked! There we were, my mother and me, sitting on the same tree trunk. I told my mum to watch the fairy ring in front of us. Once again the mist appeared with all of its little points of coloured light which gradually became fairies, all moving and dancing. My mum's eyes filled with tears but she was not unhappy. She was staring in wonder because I don't think she had ever seen fairies before in all of her life.

This time there was something a bit different as we watched. I was aware of that really lovely warm, tingling feeling again, and I looked at my mum to ask if she felt it, and I saw her surrounded by the loveliest greeny-bluey light. She really looked like a fairy herself as it shimmered over her.

Then later, the light had gone and the fairies were once again coming together in their mist. We watched as they left us and I said a little 'thank you' to them in my head. I knew they had done my mum good - they had made her better and we got up and I held her hand as we walked through the wood, back to the gardens of people.

FRED

I was scared - no use saying I wasn't. The idea of joining the army and fighting for your country had seemed a good one at the time. Thing was 'the time' had been when I was with my mates in the Dragon pub, playing dominoes and having a few pints! Oh yes, beer gives you courage - Dutch courage I think they call it. Also being in a gang of mates, helps to make you talk big. I know - I always did! What I could do and did do!

Then of course, on your own, it was a different story. Especially if you were on your way to work, and some big lout, on his way to work, gave you a hard stare! Oh, it was different then! I suppose at the bottom of me I was a bit of a softie really.

Anyway there I was, not just in the army but in France. Not just in France but in the trenches! We had only been in France a couple of hours - and on the move. We didn't realise we were on the move to the trenches. Most of us thought we would be given a bit of a warm up - some sort of settling in time. Of course there were the 'know-alls' amongst us who said we'd be straight in - and I'm sorry to have to say it, but they were right. Straight in! What a shock to a lot of us, and especially to me!

It was a strange going on in those trenches. Officers had little lean-to's made up for them where they could do paper work. Fancy paper work in war trenches! Also there were radios going, with messages coming in, and soldiers, coming in jeeps and motor bikes and, it seemed, any old thing they could get moving at some speed, forever coming and going, rushing around with bits of paper from our trench to another in a different part of the country.

Then there would be almighty great bursts of gunfire and blasting with grenades and bombs and such. People you were talking to not long before would be crumpled up, dead or badly wounded and then stretchers would appear and carry them off. What a scene!

Then, along with my mates and our battalion, we were sent down to the front trenches - that's when I really got scared. I didn't want to know about defending my country then. It wasn't my country I was defending, it seemed to me - I was abroad. I had never been abroad until now, and here I was expected to lie down on my belly and shoot anything that moved across a field or two. I wasn't that keen on killing anybody - German or whatever.

We had been shown some horrible pictures at our camp cinema in England - pictures of the Nazis and what they were doing to our lads who'd had the misfortune to get captured. Also to the Jews who, for some reason, they didn't like. I tried to get these horrible scenes into my mind to help me feel like having a go at them, but I really didn't believe them. After all films were films. We saw plenty of them at the cinema in civvy street before we were called up.

I was thinking these things, when there was a sudden deafening crash - like a very loud thunder storm -thumping and banging above my head.

Then silence.

It was an uncanny silence - probably because the noise just before it had been so terrific. I looked to my left, my rifle still in my hands, and was horrified at the scene. Everyone was dead - just laid there still - as far as my eye could see, rows of riflemen like me, but not all in one piece.

Some were covered with bits of others - arms and legs and even heads. What an awful sight! I closed my eyes to shut it out. I didn't want to see the blood spattered bodies.

I was a long time lying there and I didn't register that the silence was going on for a long time. Perhaps I had blacked out, I don't know. I certainly know that at one stage I was thinking very strongly of my family at home - my mother and father, brothers and sister. And the cat. I thought about our back garden where my father had an allotment. He worked there whenever he got the chance. He grew some lovely stuff - fruit, veges and flowers. He used to enter competitions with his chrysanths.

Nice feller me Dad. He didn't talk much, he just got on with things. He had been in the first war, and my mother said he wasn't the same man when he got back from France. France! That brought me back and I opened my eyes again dreading what I would see.

But I didn't see it! I was in a field, yes I was, but it wasn't filled with trenches and bodies and blood, it was empty except for one bloke in a uniform like mine. His cap was off though and he had bright ginger hair. He was smoking a cigarette, and was just sat there by me. When I opened my eyes and sat up, he turned to me.

'Oh, you're awake then?' was all he said.

'Where are we?' I asked him, as I looked around me.

'Damned if I know,' he said. 'All I know was a bloody great bomb dropped in the trench and blew everything to kingdom come!'

'How did we get away then?' I asked him, feeling all around myself to see if I had been injured at all. I knew I felt all right, but sometimes you don't realise when you've injured yourself, because of other things going on.

'Beats me - I don't bloody well know, but thank God we did, that's all I can say.'

'What shall we do, d'you think?' I asked him as I got to my feet.

'I was hoping YOU'd have some idea of that when you woke up!' he said.

Just at that moment an officer came along. I don't know where he sprung from, but there he was coming towards us - and smiling even!

'There you are!' he said, as if he'd been looking especially for us.'Do you lads want to come along with me?'

'Well, sir, we're just wondering what's up.' Ginger said.

To my surprise, the officer sat down on the grass and motioned me to do the same. 'What do you remember?' he asked.

We each recounted what we remembered last in the trenches and I realised as I said my bit, that the memory was not quite as vivid as it had been. There was less blood around in my mind as I thought of it.

'Well' the officer said, 'the fact of the matter is, you were both killed by those bombs.'

There was an even bigger silence at these words, than I remembered after the bombing. I looked across at Ginger who was staring open-mouthed at the officer.

After a while Ginger said 'What about you, sir?'

'Oh, I was caught at the beginning of all this lot. I was in the first landings and we all got wiped out on the beach. Mined of course!'

At this reply Ginger and I looked at each other. I had to say something - 'Are you saying, sir, that we are all dead?'

'I am. I am saying JUST that.'

I swallowed. I felt very odd, my head was going round. I put my hands up to it just to be sure I had a head and wasn't just imagining it going round!

'Excuse me sir, but how can we be dead? We're all talking here, we've got bodies which haven't a mark on 'em, and you say we got blown up? How can we have done?'

Ginger put my own feelings into words.

'It is difficult, I know to accept this. I had the same problem, which is why I am here now, talking to you. I don't know if you had religious upbringing or not, but it seems that there are two parts to a person on the earth - one is a body and one is the spirit or soul. Our bodies have been killed by bombs but our spirits have not. Our spirits cannot die.'

'D'you mean we're all ghosts?' Ginger asked, his eyes like chapel hat pegs.

'Yes, in a way. People do think of spirits as ghosts, because they don't seem solid to them on the earth. But to each other we are solid aren't we? There's nothing wispy about us is there?'

We both felt our bodies again, Ginger even pinched his own arm and winced.

'So' the officer went on, 'you have to accept this as a fact. When you get a bit more used to the idea, I will take you back to the earth so that you can really see the difference.'

We sat for a while thinking it all out. Then Ginger stood up.

'I don't know about you,' he said, looking at me, 'but I'm game now.'

I got up as well. 'All right,' I said, 'let's go.' I think I sounded surer than I felt, but I had to know what was what.

'I'm sure you'll think it a bit odd, you lads, but you will have to each take one of my hands for this.' The officer grinned as he held out his hands.

It was an odd idea, to get hold of an officer's hand and hold on, but we did it, and I don't know what happened to Ginger, but I blacked completely out.

The next thing I knew was noise - loud and continuous noise, but a little in the distance. I opened my eyes and it was all there, the muddy fields, the long trenches with men in muddy uniforms carrying stretchers to waiting field ambulances, driven by French men and women - civilians doing their bit.

I could see the little lean-to's with officers and their messengers, snatching the odd moment to drink steaming mugs of hot sweet tea. We approached closer and no-one seemed to take any notice of our being there. We went right up to one of these officer places, and our officer suggested I put out my arm and tap the signals sergeant on the shoulder, as he scribbled words on his clip-board pad. At first I was a bit reluctant, but, swallowing hard, I stretched out my arm and brought it gently down on to the man's epaulet. My hand went straight through the shoulder - I felt nothing, just air!

'They can't see us,' our officer said. 'To them we don't exist, just as when any of your relations died, you were unable to see their spirit. Many of them go to their own funerals and none of the families ever know. You must have heard of the Spiritualists and mediums? They are more sensitive than most people, and often are able to see us or hear or feel our presence.'

'I thought they were barmy!' Ginger said, frowning.

'Yes, most people do.' the officer said 'Frankly, a lot of them are - they get carried away with the power, I suppose' he added.

'Well, have you had enough?' I had been staring around me, the scene bringing back the horror of my own experience. Somehow the officer had realised this and he again held out his hands.

Once again we were back in the empty, pleasant field. I noticed this time it had a nice little stream running through it and birds were singing.

'They were there before' the officer said to me.

I was surprised because I hadn't said anything.

'I received your thoughts,' the officer explained,'You both will have to be a bit careful now, because all of your thoughts become there for anyone to know. Although we three have all been talking using words, it isn't necessary in this state of life, as spirits. There is a great deal to learn and, if you like, we will move off to begin.'

I found my voice. 'What about our families? Aren't we allowed to see them again?'

'Of course, if that is what you want. Remember though, you will not be able to communicate with them, so it might be a bit upsetting for you.'

I looked at Ginger and he said 'Yes, I would like to see my family as well.'

Well to cut a long story short, we did visit our families and it WAS upsetting for both of us, not just me. So me and

Ginger decided we would like to get on with our training. Our officer was amused at the word and suggested that first of all wouldn't we like to get out of our uniforms, which made us feel like servicemen, and wear something more to our liking and more comfortable.

'What sort of thing - you mean civvies or shrouds?'

We all laughed for the first time, I realised, and the officer surprised us by saying 'Well, you can wear just exactly what you want. For myself I feel really comfortable in something loose, so I tend to wear a robe, a bit like an old Greek, I suppose.'

Then, as we looked at him, wondering if he was joking, he suddenly was no longer wearing his uniform, but this whitish long robe thing, with gold patterns round the bottom and sleeves. Ginger was very impressed and said so.

'Well, what do you fancy wearing?' he was asked. Then, to my amazement, without Ginger saying a word, he was wearing a Roman tunic, just to the knees, and, I must admit, he looked very good - he had good legs for such a costume.

I thought about myself and decided I would just like to wear a nice pair of slacks and a blue shirt. Well! I looked down when Ginger smiled at me, and saw that that was just what I was dressed in! Talk about magic! We were very impressed with it all and ready and raring to go.

PART SEVEN

The people you have been reading about represent the kind of experiences the majority of us on the earth will most likely have. There are others, however who have not so far been represented.

During our lives, we have free will to think and act as we wish. We are, without exception, subject to the laws of the country we live in, and most people are quite happy to stay within these laws. Our thoughts and actions generally fit in with those limits, and our lives follow predictable patterns.

There are, as we are all aware, people amongst us whose thoughts run contrary to what we call law-abiding and 'normal'. Such people are totally uncaring as to how they treat others and think only of their own desires.

Throughout their lives they go their own ways, sometimes apprehended, sometimes not, perpetrating the worst in thought and deed. No matter what treatment such people receive when brought before the law, it is only when they realise for themselves, just how anti-social are their actions, that they will begin to change.

You may have heard it said that thoughts are things, and I believe this is so. It is possible for many of us to 'sense' the thoughts and feelings of those close to us - you can tell what kind of a mood some people are in. Of course there are people who keep everything to themselves - and it would not be so easy to know what these types are thinking, or feeling.

As a clairsentient, after a time being relaxed with a person, I can often know a great deal about them. In some cases I even seem to meld with them, so that their feelings are mine for that moment. You can understand then, that the presence of someone with extremely negative energies or attitudes, would make me feel very uncomfortable. I would have to move away, or force myself to think of something more pleasant - far from that situation.

I have told how the people in this book came close and I felt the experiences as if they were happening to me.

Obviously, I would not want to have this closeness with some killer with a sick mind! I can't even read graphic newspaper accounts of terrible happenings because they cause me deep depression which clouds my day. I am sure many of you are affected in just the same way.

Everyone in Read How We Died wanted to tell their stories in a desire to help us understand death a little more, in order that we would not be so scared. Those who prey on other people, for their own desires, however, would never want to come along to help. But I feel it is important that I tell you what I have discovered about these other people - and what happened to them when they died.

I was able to meld with the 'helpers' who work constantly, trying to get negative spirits to see just what they are doing and thinking, from a different angle. These 'helpers' work in groups or 'brotherhoods' as a rule, and do everything in their power to bring such minds out of the darkness they are in. It cannot be pleasant work, it cannot be instant or even short term, but they have all the time in the world, and results are their aim.

Part Seven is about some of the rest of humanity, and what they experienced upon death.

1.

In the early years of Alan's trance, we were 'sitting' one evening, and as I watched Alan in his chair opposite me, I saw him suddenly slump down, shoulders hunched, and a strange, unpleasant feeling emanated from the transformed person of my husband.

I turned off the music and started up the tape recorder and waited for the presence to speak. There was some kind of muttering, so I asked who it was. After a while he said 'Richard'.

I asked more questions, and it transpired that Richard had been a money lender. His manner of speaking suggested

178

the seventeenth or eighteenth century.

It was difficult conversing with him. He was slow in answering me, and I was not quite sure what to ask to draw him out. In between my questions, he constantly complained of the treatment he was receiving, the permanent darkness and the people he had around him. It seemed some kind of nightmare that he could not awaken from.

He was ignored or verbally attacked; there were no friends apart from voices, or the occasional priest who visited him. He found it hard to accept the company and the words of the priest, because he himself was a Jew. Why did they not send a Rabbi to him? Why were there no pleasures in life any more?

He moaned and sighed a great deal, so I decided to ask him more about his former life. It was difficult dragging the information out of him. I asked if he realised how the extortionate interest rates charged by money lenders must have caused great suffering - leading often to suicides. Once having gone to a money lender, people could never free themselves because the loans could never be repaid.

Richard found nothing wrong with this. Every money lender charged in the same way. If people wanted to borrow money, then they had to accept the conditions. If they killed themselves it was the money lender who suffered, unless they had a family he could apply to for the rest of the repayments. He could not see that he was living off people's misery. He felt justified and blameless - even though he had applied pressures - had people beaten up and even killed, at his bidding. Everyone in his profession was the same. He was no different, he had to live.

It was very evident that there was much more he had done. I tried to persuade him to see his actions from a different view point, and suggested he lacked compassion, and that he was suffering now for all he had made others suffer, and then I stopped speaking and so ended the 'sitting'.

Almost a year later, we held a 'sitting' and a person addressed me in a friendly and courteous way. He announced himself as Richard and said I might not remember him. I have a very long memory and I did. We talked for quite a time. He was very different, no longer slouched and hunched up, and no longer complaining about his surroundings and treatment.

Somehow he had got something from our talk that had made him think. With further help from the 'voices', he had conceded to himself that he could have been wrong. From then on, the darkness lightened around him. It was not still daylight, but a kind of dusk. There was no pleasant scenery or countryside, but there were not so many unpleasant people pushing him about. He said he felt a little happier, and even managed to converse with the priest when he came.

We talked for about half an hour.

A few months later, I felt the urge to write. I sat down and knew it was Richard. I relaxed and let my pencil write the words that flowed into my mind. It was the story of Richard's life from his childhood. He had had a very normal and happy childhood, but later, for one reason or another - chiefly his love of money and the power it brought - he drifted into a very different kind of life.

The story was never completed, but it told me what I think Richard wanted me to know, and what he needed to understand about himself. It was as if the flowing of words released his feelings and compassion. I have not heard from him since, but I feel his changed state of mind will allow mention of him here.

* * * * *

2.

At a group sitting one evening, the thoughts of a man were communicated through Alan's trance. He had been in a situation that he thought could only be solved by killing someone.

Because of the circumstances surrounding his action, he was not sentenced to death, but he was confined for life in a cell six feet by four feet. The only window was a small one high up in the wall. It gave out only a little light and he was unable to see to read. There was no other light in his cell.

His food was pushed through a grill; no-one spoke to him; he was never allowed out. He had nothing but his thoughts. He spent thirty two years in this cell and then he died.

As far as he was concerned, he was totally unaware of his death. In life he had lost track of time, apart from the ritual of his food being brought. So, even now, some forty years or more since he died, he is still in his cell, living his ritual, still thinking his thoughts, totally unable to realise his freedom.

Eventually, someone will get through to him, and no doubt the shock will render him unconscious for a while.

* * * *

3.

The man was scared for the first time in his life. The jailers roughly pulled him towards the scaffold. All around people were waiting for him to be hung. Not for him to die. No, they wanted the opportunity to get their revenge. How he hated them all! He could hear the cat calls and his face stung as well-aimed rotten eggs exploded, the foul stench causing him to reech. There was the occasional raucous laughter as eggs hit the two burly men dragging him along.

They pushed him up the steps, kicking him when he held back, and one of them put the rope around his neck. He stood there shaking, and the crowd pelted him with rotten fruit, filth and stones. The jailers allowed this to go on for some time, to amuse the crowd more. Then it happened. The board beneath him fell and he with it. At that moment a sharp pain and he felt as if his head had exploded.

They were on him like hounds on a fox.

So much was happening but far away, as if he was above watching it all. He could still think and he was still hating them. He waited to die. He did not die. Instead he saw them

181

all clawing at him, pulling him down, cutting open his belly. People were laughing, holding up pieces of his flesh, dripping with his blood and throwing it to dogs to eat. Flies in droves were covering his widely gaping body.

The man still experiences this same ritual - over and over again. He remembers his crimes. He remembers how he cut up the bellies of his victims - weak men, women and children, who came easily into his power. There was some kind of sadistic pleasure in watching the terror he caused.

Now, none of it will go away - he never sleeps. Eventually he will pass into unconsciousness, when he can no longer bear to watch his actions - the lowest men can get. Then it will be a new start. He will be amongst people again in a very limited sense - to see how he will treat them. That, however will be far in his future.

* * * *

4.

The scene is a stark, grey, misty plain. There is a lone building, not a cottage, more of a hut. A few yards in front of the building, a solitary figure is sitting on a boulder, staring at a depression in the ground, holding a very small amount of murky, stagnant water. There are one or two misshapen, leafless trees, but that is all.

The mist never lifts. It is always half light. There are no sounds, just a dull, eerie silence. There are never any people - apart from the visitors from time to time.

The man's face is gaunt. He must have been handsome during his life. That would have been when he spent his time as a very smart confidence trickster. All his life he had cheated people. He specialised in finding rich, lonely women. He was charming to them until they had married him, then he had found many ways of driving them insane - even to suicide.

He was always so clever in his plans. He set up strong alibis and was never caught. Six women had died and three were in asylums when he, himself suddenly had a heart attack.

Oh, it was a bad one. A sharp stabbing pain in his arm and then quickly a terrific overwhelming pain in his chest. It was soon over though.

The trouble was, when he opened his eyes after the bursting in his ear drums, he found himself here. No-one ever came here, he could not count the visitors - missionaries as he thought of them.

In his life, he had never got on with his fellow men - always women. He thought men might see through him, so he kept well away from them. Same with those missionaries who came to visit him here - they certainly saw through him, so no point in talking to them.

For the millionth time he wondered how long he would have to stay here. It was getting difficult to even think now. He had tried to conjure things up in his mind, but all he ever saw were replays of those women looking at him - so trusting, loving and grateful! They were right to be grateful - who else had taken pains to flatter them, wait on them......and oh yes! He was sexually so good with them, they were soon eating out of his hands.....well, at the beginning.

That is as far as his thoughts would ever go. Just like his surroundings. His world was very small, drab and extremely lonely.

THE END

Further copies of this book can be obtained from

Andrea Grieveson,
P.O.Box 25,
Wrexham,
LL14 6WD.

At £7.95 including post and packing.
Cheques and postal orders made payable to A.Grieveson.